GO COACH
YOURSELF

GO COACH YOURSELF

A HANDBOOK FOR
HAPPINESS AND
INNER STRENGTH

FRUMMA ROSENBERG-GOTTLIEB

MEDIA

Published 2025 by Gildan Media LLC
aka G&D Media
www.GandDmedia.com

Front cover design by David Rheinhardt of Pyrographx

Interior design by Meghan Day Healey of Story Horse, LLC

Library of Congress Cataloging-in-Publication Data is available upon request

ISBN: 978-1-7225-0714-5

10 9 8 7 6 5 4 3 2 1

Contents

PART TWO

People Who Love People　109

Introduction

Self-Coaching: The Backstory

There's no getting around it. No matter how privileged or oppressed any one of us may seem to be, the verdict is unanimous: life is hard. We can allow it to beat us to a pulp. Yet life can grant us wisdom, make us strong, teach us lessons. The second option requires determination and skills, which can be acquired and fortified with every loss as well as every win. These skills can enable us to become adept at transforming posttraumatic stress into posttraumatic growth, negative self-image into positivity and confidence, unhappiness into joy. I call this *self-coaching*.

I love self-coaching, because it's free! It's also empowering, because we learn to trust ourselves, our inner wisdom, and our ability to connect to our higher selves. As a professional coach over many decades, I've often witnessed the enormous value that accrues when a coaching client works with a trained coach. But that is not always possible. Moreover, there are additional and profound advantages to becoming one's own coach.

That is why I wrote this book. I believe we are all capable of mastering the art of becoming better today than we were yesterday. And I am excited to share with you the coaching tools I have acquired.

We are all capable of mastering the art of becoming better today than we were yesterday. And I am excited to share with you the coaching tools I have acquired.

My personal journeys, on high roads and low roads, have molded me into a loving matriarch of a large family, an effective educator, and a compassionate coach. I'll spare you the many details—this book is not about me; and anyway, no two of us are the same. But I will share some of my highlights with you, because knowing how I got where I am today can be useful, even for those who have come from what might as well have been a different universe. The particulars of any one person's story are of value not so much for the drama as for the insights we might glean and apply in our own lives.

I grew up entitled—very entitled, which was fine until I had to actually grow up. I was the cherished only child of educated, refined parents. They doted on me and helped me develop a positive self-image, which was terrific, but there was a downside. In the same breath they also taught me to be exceedingly conscious of other people's opinions. When I came home from a party brimming with excitement and new stories to share, the first question Mom would invariably ask was, "How did they think you looked?"

My mother's favorite bedtime story was *The Little Engine That Could*. Most kids of my generation grew up with the same story, all about an anthropomorphic train who volunteered for a job that was way above its pay grade, delivering toys to the boys and girls on the other side of the mountain. The little engine succeeded because he coached himself incessantly with a powerful affirmation: "I think I can, I think I can." The book was a perennial hit on every elementary school's best-seller list, but no one loved it like my mom. It became my mantra: "I think I can, I think I can."

My father was a superbly ethical stockbroker who never quit anything he began. He passed that value on to me, as well as a love of gardening, aesthetics, good music, and dance. He taught me that happiness was about being whole. He could deal with the stress of the ticker tapes of Wall Street because he under-stood something he would call "recovery time." Relaxing in his gardens, long walks on the beach, playing the ukulele, and dancing to the old standards were commitments that were no less firm than his early morning commute on the train across the river to his downtown Manhattan office.

In September, after we had clipped back the prize dahlias and fertilized the flower beds, Dad and I would mull over the bulb catalogs from Holland and choose the perfect blend of tulips for the spring: yellows, pinks, deep purples, double-petaled and linen-textured whites. In early May, when the tulips were in bloom, passersby would stop their cars in front of our home to take pictures.

Everything my father did, he did artfully. He was slender and graceful, and dressed with close attention to a style that reminded me of Fred Astaire. How well I remember dancing with him, gliding across the diamonds embedded in the side-walks as we left the theater. We never missed a good musical. In his later years he took off on Wednesdays. He valued self-care and made it an essential part of his every week.

In my parents' lovely home by the sea, there was a beautifully carved bronze Chinese bell, occupying a conspicuous place on the dining room table. Whenever my mother rang the bell, Marie would come in from the kitchen with trays of steaming hot delicacies that she had lovingly prepared. Marie was always smiling, except when she was chewing a fresh wad of tobacco, at which times she had a puckered look on her deeply lined, almost leathery face. She sang while she was doing the laundry or ironing my father's shirts with just the right hint of starch; and she chawed while cleaning and dusting and puffing up the gray and pink calico pillows on my bed. She was happy in our house. She had never married, and we were good company. My parents enjoyed her stories of growing up in Mississippi and learning to read in a one-room schoolhouse. They respected her work ethic and were charmed by her love for the gospel songs of her youth. Often, when she was humming in the sunroom, my Mom would sing along with her. There was never an undertone of prejudice or position—just mutual respect and appreciation. When my parents donated their share to charity, they were just as excited about building a playground for the black kids in Marie's community as in contributing to our temple. I was a stranger to racial discrimination and anti-Semitism. Marie lived securely with us for many years. So did the bronze bell.

When I was twenty, I married my first husband, Joel. He was my high-school sweetheart, a handsome lifeguard with an athletic build. But there was a lot more than good looks. He was a sensitive soul, an idealist. He came from a very different world. His parents were rough around the edges, high-school graduates, salt of the earth. His dad made his fortune as a rum runner and later in black market gas and lower-middle-class rentals.

My parents recognized Joel as a diamond in the rough but nonetheless not so subtly suggested that I go to Europe for a year to cool down before doing anything rash. But I was crazy about his idealism, his well-muscled body, and the freckles on his nose. We got engaged on the Fourth of July. I wore a Seal Chapman black chiffon dress and a string of pearls my mother had purchased in Curaçao on her most recent cruise. His mom was wearing a chunky gold charm bracelet, and his dad was smoking a fat cigar. It didn't make a difference. I was madly in love.

We were married the following May and shortly thereafter flew off to the enchanted island of Kauai as Volunteers in Service to America. I asked Mom if I could take the bronze bell to my new home. I set it down in a place of honor on my dining room table.

But when I rang the bell, no one came.

It was there in Hawaii that I began to discover spirituality. The world's most breathtaking landscapes and the sweet smell of adventure quickened my heart; the pristine waterfalls nestled into mountainsides of blooming ginger and plumeria, and the vast expanse of the aquamarine Pacific Ocean opened my inner eye. With an assist from the late-night campfires among some of the original Haight-Ashbury flower children, plus a psychedelic experience or two, I was ready to become a believer.

Back on the mainland, we spent colorful years as pioneers in the hippie movement and the owners of one of America's first natural food stores, in Boulder, Colorado. We lived in a log cabin without electricity or running water on the western slopes of the Rocky Mountains. We ate a strictly vegan diet and meditated twice a day. We owned fifty acres of organic orchards nestled in the foothills of snowcapped, majestic mountains. To the west of our farm were seventy-five miles of national wilderness. The elk and moose used to visit occasionally to nibble on our fruit trees. Our house guests included Yogi Bhajan, the Hog Farm, and Shlomo Carlebach, the singing rabbi. We were hot stuff in the wild, wide world of kindred souls seeking enlightenment.

Gone were the days when Sunday drivers would cruise by my parents' house to take pictures of the perfect rows of Dutch tulips. Our Colorado scene attracted a different sort of pilgrim, looking for a campsite or a guru or a safe set and setting for their first dance with magic mushrooms. They were young and idealistic, thirsty for truth, emotionally needy, and mostly confused. I took on the Wendy role to Peter Pan's lost boys. Not incidentally, I also became the mother of my first two children.

One might say that was my first serious coaching training. It was during those wilderness years that I developed a passionate interest in emotional intelligence, though it wasn't called that yet. Neither had "positive psychology" yet matured into a formal field of study. Nonetheless, as I sat nursing my sons, I assiduously read every book I could get my hands on that explored those concepts.

The Path Becomes Personal

As we began to outgrow the log cabin lifestyle, we started thinking about the kids' education. Our boys were getting older, and our Rocky Mountain paradise was clearly not going to offer them the sort of stability we had envisioned. When my husband went back to graduate school and set his sights on a PhD in anthropology, it began to dawn on us that anthropology represents more than simply an academic discipline with opportunities to do fieldwork in exotic places. For the anthropologist who takes his training to heart, the in-depth study of other cultures can lead to a more meaningful experience of one's own life and family values, seen through the lens of one's ancestral heritage. We recognized the importance of connecting with a well-defined, well-rooted culture that would prove ethical, spiritual, and sustainable. The quest for emotional intelligence and spiritual growth eventually, perhaps inevitably, calls for developing a sense of history, connection, and continuity.

The quest for emotional intelligence and spiritual growth eventually, perhaps inevitably, calls for developing a sense of history, connection, and continuity.

I'll share here a glimpse into how my personal self-coaching journey has been enhanced by the wisdom embedded in the cultural origins of the family I come from. We all come from somewhere. I want to encourage you to connect with your own origins. I've observed that the more solidly rooted we are in our various legacies, histories, and traditions, the more powerfully and effectively we can blaze our personal trails as we learn to guide ourselves going forward. That suggestion may be at least as important as the self-coaching tools I'm offering in this book.

All my life I had turned my back on my Judaism as something stagnant and legalistic. In the synagogue of my youth, I never felt connected to a Higher Power. To my surprise, however, that was about to change. A series of events, too long a story to recount in these pages, brought us back east to the home of a charismatic Parisian family who were not only luminaries in the world of natural foods and alternative healing but also the progeny of an illustrious line of Moroccan Jewish rabbis of great renown.

We spent our first authentic Shabbat with them, along with several other young American refugees from the sixties scene we knew so well, kindred spirits whose search for meaning resonated with ours. The home was filled with ancient mystic melodies and the rich aromas of North African cuisine. The family warmth and wholeness were palpable. I lit the Sabbath candles and was overtaken by a feeling of belonging, of finding my truth. But beyond the exhilaration of that initial exotic experience, there was a sense of connection to a truth that was not just *my* truth. It felt, if I may be so bold, universal, eternal. It seemed so right that it was worth a shot.

After Shabbat we called my husband's graduate advisor to ascertain the deadline for his PhD dissertation. He was given seven years' leeway. Then we called the manager of our health food business in Colorado (by then it had become a chain of stores) and asked him to take over for a while. The next call was to some friends who had always wanted to buy our land. We went back, packed up our belongings, and said heartfelt farewells to the hundred-year-old log cabin, the organic fruit orchards, and my beloved horses. We kissed the earth, turned eastward again, and never looked back.

We got serious about our Jewish roots and went to study in a school designed specifically for newbies like us. We introduced a commitment to Sabbath observance in our lives. I learned how to read Hebrew so I could pray daily from a traditional prayer book. I traded in my embroidered jeans and hiking boots for dresses with long sleeves and a scarf on my head. I started studying the Five Books of Moses, the Prophets, and the Code of Jewish Law. I began using the Hebrew name that had been given to me at birth, though having ignored it for the first twenty-eight years of my life, I had to ask my mom what it was. Frumma. My God, it sounded like something straight out of *Fiddler on the Roof*! But I got used to it, just as I did with kashrut (kosher observance) and all the holidays I had never heard of.

In the decades that followed, as I established my professional roles as educator, mentor, and coach, I realized that although connection with the traditional ways and wisdom of forebears is an essential component of a meaningful life, there is also such a thing as too much, too soon. Those were days of precipitous change for our generation. There's not even an iota of regret, but I've learned a thing or two since then (some of which we'll no doubt be discussing in the pages to come).

We became codirectors of a spiritual drop-in center for college students, a Chabad House, reaching out to teach Torah values and Jewish customs to people who wanted to learn under the aegis of Menachem Mendel Schneerson, the Lubavitcher

Rebbe, the best-known Hasidic leader of his generation. I was the event planner, spiritual advisor, chief cook, bottle washer, and go-to girl for practical guidance through the chaotic maze of modernity. It was a good life, clean and elevating. I felt settled, grounded, and yet simultaneously connected to the higher realms. My children had structure and morality.

Judaism encourages large families and generous hospitality. I (eventually) had seven children, and through it all there was always lots of company for Shabbat dinner. (But the bell didn't bring food to the table the way it had in my mother's dining room.) In addition to paying the bills, I had to figure out how to be organized, personable, and relaxed in my 24/7 roles as mother, caterer, teacher, and emotional anchor. *Order* would prove to be the key to my survival, and it didn't come easily.

We moved around a lot. My husband was one of the sincerest guys in the universe, an innovator, and a dreamer, but he could also be a bull in a china shop and managed to piss off a lot of people wherever we went. We had our share of financial challenges and kept looking for a workable solution that would be spiritually uplifting as well.

There were many startups and a lot of shattered dreams. Although we moved back and forth between urban and rural environments, the geographic fixes weren't working. No one had yet coined the label ADHD, so I had no context in which to understand my partner's highly enthusiastic but erratic behavior. I couldn't handle the tension that was building at home. My search for more and more self-help books became increasingly desperate and futile. I attended classes that promised to cultivate equanimity; I became a gym rat, hoping to dance away the unpleasant emotions.

I went to therapy. *He* went to therapy. *We* went to therapy. Failure wasn't in my job description, but fail is what we eventually did. It was a turbulent divorce that took seven years to complete, and all the while I could hear my mother asking, "How did they think you looked?"

During my years as a single parent, my oldest daughter was diagnosed with a debilitating mental illness. She moved back home with two babies under three, so instead of raising my three youngest children on my own, I was now caring for six— exhausted, embarrassed, impoverished, defeated. The Sabbath and the holidays that had once been the happiest days of my life now became the saddest. I convinced myself that everyone was talking about me behind my back, and though it certainly wasn't true, in my own eyes I had become the world's biggest loser, a total train wreck.

But I never forgot that Little Engine who always knew he could. I could too, so I did. I climbed out of the hole and took charge of my life, changing my perspective until every obstacle became a thought-provoking challenge rather than an insurmountable hurdle. JFK, my hero of college days, had long before made an indelible impression on me when he said, "Those who dare to fail miserably can achieve greatly." Having cornered the market on failure, I now knew it was high time to achieve.

Many of the tools I employ today to help my students and coaching clients were honed in those hard-knocks days. I began to keep a journal and a daily gratefulness notebook. I went back to the gym four or five times a week. I committed to a food program and lost fifteen pounds of sad memories that had been masquerading as cheesecake. I purchased a four-part CD course from time management guru Stephen Covey.

And that Little Engine kept chugging in the background. "I think I can, I think I can." I advanced from being a teacher to team leader, to vice principal, to principal. I felt fit and financially secure. The kids were growing up healthy and happy. My oldest daughter got back on her feet, albeit a bit wobbly, and became able to live on her own.

At age sixty-one, I met Mr. Right (most of the time). His name is Simcha, which means *joy* or *happiness* in Hebrew. That's not without some irony in that his personal challenge for most of his life had been to live up to the promise of his name (as he doesn't hesitate to admit). Meanwhile, my own test became learning how to step back and allow him to heal his own almost-broken heart from within. Because, as any coach worth her salt will tell you, genuine happiness is something every one of us must earn, and own. No matter how loving the relationship and how deep the bond, no one can make anyone else happy. This is one place where that old platitude about having the wisdom to know the difference between what we can change and what we cannot is not a platitude at all. As we'll see, it becomes all the more pertinent when we're coaching ourselves.

To make the match still more interesting, both of us had struggled from time to time with earning our respective livelihoods. A mutual friend, when she heard we were engaged, called to congratulate me. In her candid and sarcastic style, knowing a bit about my fiancé's somewhat dicey financial status, she said, "He's a great guy. And this is obviously not a marriage of convenience."

As of this writing, we've been lovingly married for seventeen years, have traveled the world, renovated our home, and written a book together. He supported my choice to leave the nine-to-five grind and become a life coach. I probably wouldn't have had the nerve to do so without him. In addition to convincing me that romantic love isn't reserved for the young and glamorous, Simcha is a lifelong learner, a scholar and poet and mentor to many. He has shown me that the window for personal transformation doesn't close when you are forty or fifty or sixty. Old dogs can indeed learn new tricks. He thinks it would be wonderful if I were to decide to complete my doctorate in psychology sometime after my eightieth birthday. We are helpers and healers in our own community and are frequently called upon to give talks and workshops on emotional intelligence, mindfulness, and happiness.

The Power of Allowing

Although it is marvelous to have a skillful coach who listens attentively and empathetically and knows how to ask penetrating questions, much of coaching can be successfully self-led. That's what I want to share with you in this book: the core philosophies, exercises, and (for lack of a better term) rituals I have found effective in my personal journey.

People often ask me, knowing how I've worn so many different hats in my various careers, what I do *now*. Winston Churchill once said that success is stumbling from one failure to another without losing enthusiasm. I've done my share of that—not necessarily failing but realizing that what I had been doing just didn't float my boat. I've been a pioneer in the natural foods industry, an educator, a relationship coach, a meditation teacher, a spiritual counselor, an addiction therapist, a high-school principal, an aerobics teacher, a horse trainer, a community developer, an events planner, and a public speaker. (Probably left out a few.) When I tell people I'm now a certified happiness coach, they shoot me a skeptical look, like, "Seriously? That's it? Kind of, er, superficial, no?"

Umm, no. Happiness is the ultimate commodity, not just in and of itself but in the ways it generates and nurtures innumerable positive qualities. Try these on for starters: kindness; resilience; enthusiasm; creativity; improved problem-solving skills; the courage to try new things; tranquility; stronger relationships; a less judgmental attitude; even a strengthened immune system. Who would you be with all that at hand?

Happiness is the ultimate commodity, not just in and of itself but in the ways it generates and nurtures innumerable positive qualities.

That awesome person is my idea of ideal. Happiness, and the wholeness it engenders, is what I want for myself, my loved ones, and my clients. That is why I've been studying emotional intelligence and positive psychology all my adult life. I am confident that EQ, an assessment of emotional intelligence (rather than mere IQ, measuring only one's intelligence quotient), is the most accurate predictor of success and well-being. And the most essential item on that menu is happiness.

My personal trainer talks about happiness in terms of its benefits for physical fitness. My inspirational coach, Dr. Tal Ben-Shahar, created a course on happiness that became Harvard's most popular and highly attended class. My spiritual guide, Rabbi Menachem Schneerson, often quoted sacred texts extoling the power of happiness, emphasizing how happiness breaks all boundaries. My husband and children tell me that I'm so much more pleasant and fun to be around when I'm happy. Harvard alumnus Shawn Achor, a positive psychology advocate and esteemed professor at Harvard who is another well-known proponent of positive psychology, cites research indicating that physicians who cultivate happiness in their personal lives are 19 percent more accurate in their diagnoses. (Board certification is no longer my number one criterion when choosing a new doctor.)

Wholeness creates happiness. Tal Ben-Shahar uses the acronym *SPIRE* as comprising the wellness of a whole human being. It stands for *Spiritual well-being, Physical well-being, Intellectual well-being, Relational well-being, and Emotional well-being.* I've studied it, I've practiced it, I've researched it and "me-searched" it. I've coached it. I've compiled it into this book so you can coach yourself to be a happier, more effective person. You might want to be healthier or wealthier or improve your relationships at home or at the office. You can pick and choose which practices you think will work for you. Don't knock them till you try them. Take them on in stages; master one practice, then add another; apply them and accumulate them until they become the habits that define you. I would love to help you have it all.

There is a Tibetan folktale about a nomad who embarks on a long journey along rough and rocky roads. To protect his bare feet, he collects the hides of dead animals, which he laboriously skins and scrapes and spreads on the path ahead of him to make it more bearable. This takes forever, and he is not getting very far when he has a revolutionary insight. If he takes the hide of one animal and makes himself a pair of shoes, every place he steps will be more pleasant.

We can't change the world we inhabit from painful to comfortable, but we can change our garments and change ourselves. It would be foolish to think we could protect ourselves from every obstacle on our path, but we can strengthen ourselves and find the right tools to cope with the world around us.

Although our goal is to become happier, more effective individuals, I would be doing a disservice to lead you down the "happily ever after" road. Happy people aren't always happy. As I write this, I am on my dream vacation, but this morning I woke up absolutely miserable. It was a combination of First World problems, like figuring out how to make the water hot in the Jacuzzi and where to get a decent cup of java, along with a much deeper, devastating, gnawing feeling that I'm still not good enough (and nor is my guy). We should be accomplishing so much more—bigger successes, fame, and fortune. I often self-sabotage by comparing myself to superstars of one type or another. Instead of celebrating my past victories, I ask myself why I am not as productive, effective, and daring today as I seemed to be *then*. Fortunately, I have learned how to bounce back (most of the time). I understand that negative thoughts and feelings are always right there, close to the surface. We oscillate between self-love and self-loathing. It's part of the game.

Life is filled with ups and downs. But there are really no such things as positive and negative emotions. There are painful and pleasant emotions, and all emotions are acceptable. Anger, anxiety, shame, fear, or sadness are all legitimate. The complications arise when we act on our feelings inappropriately.

By learning to coach yourself, your emotional intelligence will improve. You will be able to recognize and regulate your emotions. *If you can name them, you can tame them.* You will become more sensitive to your emotional terrain, as well as to that of the people you interact with. Your impulse control will be strengthened; you'll grow better able to proactively respond to the challenges in your life that bring on those unpleasant emotions. You'll understand how to accept and work through an emotion, then move on, rather than suppressing it and pretending it doesn't exist, only to pay the price later. You will find that you squander less energy in staying stuck and ruminating on those same stultifying moments.

We begin by allowing ourselves to be human. When we attempt to quash our emotions, it's like someone saying, *no matter what, do not think about the pink elephant.* Which of course makes the pink elephant ever more present in our minds.

Victor Frankl, the much-respected psychiatrist and author of *Man's Search for Meaning,* tells us to *encourage* the painful emotions. By embracing and accepting feelings like anxiety, fear, or sadness, we can work through them and get to the other side. Frankl calls this the *Theory of Paradoxical Intentions.* Ignoring our emotions is like ignoring gravity. Like it or not, gravity is a part of our reality. Like it or not, we'll have gloomy days and murky moods. We'll be jealous of that beautiful, charismatic woman, resent the colleague who just got promoted, angry at a best friend or spouse. And dammit, those horrific feelings just keep popping up. Why? Because we can't ignore emotions, even though we've convinced ourselves they are unacceptable.

Our ideal behavior, as we're well aware, ought to be an expression of kindness, refinement, and sensitivity to the needs of loved ones. But our emotions don't always match up. We may envy them, be irritated with them, or simply dislike them. It's normal. What's not so obvious, however, is that when we try to block or suppress painful emotions, we're also smothering the ups as well as the downs, putting a blanket on our *pleasurable* feelings.

When I was in college, I discovered the writings of Kahlil Gibran and walked around with a copy of his most popular book, *The Prophet,* in my backpack. Having discovered this not yet popular piece of esoteric literature, I thought I was cool. It complemented my carefully cultivated counterculture image—an oversized khaki jacket from the army-navy store, combat boots, and long hair flowing down my back.

As of today, *The Prophet* has sold more than ten million copies, making Gibran one of the three best-selling poets in the world. Gibran lyrically addresses the interdependent features of joy and sadness:

> *Your joy is your sorrow unmasked.*
> *And the selfsame well from which your laughter*
>   *rises was oftentimes filled with your tears.*
> *And how else can it be?*
> *The deeper that sorrow carves into your being,*
>   *the more joy you can contain.*

And yet we muzzle our unpleasant emotions, trying to block them out and distract ourselves. In fear of our feelings, we drive ourselves further from the place we are meant to be, most commonly today into the world of electronic devices and virtual reality. Antidepressants are now prescribed as casually as antibiotics. Most people don't realize how those magical tablets numb us to the possibility of happiness just as powerfully as they purport to soothe our miseries. It's OK to cry ourselves to sleep from time to time, or to share our pain and our fears with good friends. It is magnificently human.

This week, for thirty minutes each day, pay attention to what you're feeling, and simply *allow* yourself to feel what it is you're feeling. If it hurts, don't try to change it. Don't reject it, don't fight it. Simply surrender to the emotion and allow it to flow through you. If and when the feeling changes, in whatever direction, allow yourself to continue to flow with the change.

PART ONE

Your Inner Strength Handbook

1

Rituals: Not Quite Clockwork, but Close

We are what we repeatedly do.
Excellence, then, is not an act, but a habit.
—ARISTOTLE

Deep within the human mind lives a mighty desire for orderliness, consistency, and schedule. It's a quality that is embedded in nature, of course. The sun and the moon rise and set with stunning regularity. The seasons come and go with a predictable rhythm. So it is not surprising that our bodies perform best when they rest, awaken, and eat at the same time from day to day.

Does this sound dull to you? It is in fact liberating, downright empowering. We have more important things to think about than necessary but everyday tasks. When these basics are so well scheduled they become automatic, we are more likely to live up to our full potential. Chaos confines us; constancy frees us. If you crave such constancy, or at the very least think it's a good idea, there is no better tool than the judicious use of rituals.

Many of us are uncomfortable with the concept of rituals, thinking of them as merely symbolic gestures that are performed by rote and don't accomplish much. I beg to differ: Rituals support our long-term visions and goals by incorporating beneficial actions into our everyday lives. They are precise and meaningful behaviors, motivated by deeply held values, and performed at specific times for maximum effect. They support our higher purpose, so we should consider them nonnegotiable. For example, you may not have grown up flossing your teeth regularly, but now you do it every morning. It becomes automatic, because you have bought into the principle that reducing plaque makes for a healthier mouth (and heart).

Far from stifling us with rigid behaviors, rituals facilitate inspiration. Tal Ben-Shahar addressed this idea in his bestselling book *Happier: Learn the Secrets to Daily Joy and Lasting Fulfillment*: "The most creative individuals—whether artists, businesspeople or parents—have rituals that they follow. Paradoxically, the routine frees them up to be creative." Top athletes have rituals: they know that at specific hours every day they're on the field, then in the gym, and then they stretch and take a hot shower. Successful writers set aside a certain amount of time each day to write, and they make it non-negotiable.

We need to take a similar approach toward the changes we want to introduce. By developing good habits and practicing them each day, you affirm that you have control over the core of your life amid all the chaos.

By developing good habits and practicing them each day, you affirm that you have control over the core of your life amid all the chaos.

James Clear made it to the best-seller list with his book *Atomic Habits: An Easy and Proven Way to Build Good Habits and Break Bad Ones*. He explains how the positive effects of small actions compound over time. If you can become 1 percent better each day, your results will be thirty-seven times better after one year. The impact created by a change in habits is like the effect of adjusting the route of a plane by a few degrees. If a plane takes off from Los Angeles heading to New York, an adjustment as small as 3.5 degrees will change the destination to Washington, D.C. instead.

This means that by taking baby steps, making simple, realistic, but minor adjustments and increasing gradually over time, you will eventually produce significant change. I'm not going to become a long-distance runner this week, but I can get closer to my vision by dedicating ten minutes at a specific time each day to walking out the front door and around the block.

Some helpful baby steps can be even quicker than ten minutes. Behavioral scientists and business coaches speak of a process called *minimal viable interventions* (MVIs)—strategies or actions designed to create a meaningful and often substantial improvement by making the smallest possible effective change. It's a concept borrowed from an idea that's grown popular in the tech startup world, the *minimum viable product* (MVP), which focuses on launching products designed with just enough novel features to satisfy new users and keep them coming back for more.

Because we know that too much sitting is considered as harmful today as smoking was in years gone by, we need to do something to keep us healthy as we constrict ourselves into forty-hour workweeks (or worse). If you stand up from the chair every hour or two, do ten jumping jacks, run in place, or some other brief and easy exercise, you'll enjoy benefits beyond your imagination—and you won't be overwhelmed by complex or time-consuming routines that you simply can't sustain. Some trainers call these *microworkouts*.

Incorporate short bursts of exercise at convenient times throughout the day, such as a five-minute stretching routine in the morning, a brief walk during a lunch break, or a few minutes of bodyweight exercises like squats or push-ups in the evening. Park at the far end of the lot to increase your steps; take the stairs instead of the elevator; gift yourself with a few minutes of stretching before bed. Tiny, atomic, health-related habits will make a huge difference when applied consistently over time.

When you exercise, even briefly, your body goes into action mode, and your brain triggers the release of endorphins. These are neurotransmitters: chemical messengers that transmit transformative signals within the nervous system. Endorphins act as natural painkillers and mood elevators. When released, they bind to specialized receptors in areas of your brain associated with emotions and pain perception. This interaction can reduce pain and trigger positive feelings, even sometimes a sense of euphoria, often called a "runner's high." Endorphins can also help ease stress, alleviate anxiety, and contribute to an overall sense of well-being. That's why after a good workout, many people feel happier, more relaxed, and energized from the release of these natural mood-boosting chemicals. Imagine dipping into this runner's high in the midst of a busy workday. After a microworkout, your thinking will be clearer, and you'll face your next task with new enthusiasm.

What sort of rituals would make you happier, more purposeful, energetic, and effective? Ten minutes of meditation? Reading for pleasure for thirty minutes a day? Date night with your spouse? Yoga? Introducing MVIs into your workday?

Once you identify a ritual you'd like to try, write it down and begin your commitment. New rituals may be difficult at first, so remember Clear's advice: keep them atomic—short and simple. Don't introduce more than one or two at a time. Within three weeks or a month, they will become as automatic as brushing your teeth. Make sure a ritual becomes a habit before you introduce a new one.

Habits, they say, are difficult to break. With good habits, that's good news. As you coach yourself in establishing life-supporting rituals, you will realize that *every act of self-control is an act of self-respect*. This is one of my favorite affirmations. It often pushes me into my workout clothes on a lazy morning. Write it on the bathroom mirror, print it on a little card and attach it to your keys, or design it as your screen saver. It's powerful, and so are you!

The Habit Stack

Energy is usually at its peak during the first part of your day; which means you should be completing habits in the morning that inspire or excite you about the day ahead.

—S. J. Scott, *Habit Stacking*

Replacing a few negative habits with positive habits can easily make the difference between being mostly unhappy and being happy most of the time. If introducing one purposeful ritual is a good idea, imagine the benefit of constructing a meaning-ful daily regimen of several practices that cover *all* the bases. A stack of habits that encompasses all aspects of daily life, from physical health to spiritual well-being and back again, can make *getting better all the time* as much a part of you as washing your face in the morning. It's doable. The key is to methodically and consistently link together small, easily accomplished, routine practices that naturally belong together.

1. Choose two—and only two—rituals or disciplines that you know will contribute to your happiness, health, or success if you do them every day. Yoga? Swimming? Prayer? Abdom-inal crunches? Learning a new language or a new instru-ment? Sunbathing or stargazing? Select whichever two will work for you, ones that will enhance each other and fit together logically.

2. Establish a time when you can do them each day and stick with it. It may be first thing in the morning when the birds are chirping, or a late evening routine when the world is more likely to leave you in peace. If you can keep to a consis-tent starting time for at least a month, your stack will gain momentum.

3. Limit the allotted time: do your two activities for only five minutes each. Does that seem like a cop-out? No! You're not being a wimp; you're guaranteeing that you won't spin out. You're astutely easing into excellence.

4. Make a daily commitment, make it non-negotiable, and show up. If you miss a day, don't quit, and certainly don't beat yourself up. Just try to return to your intention as quickly as possible.

5. Add one minute to each activity each week. Yes, just *one minute* per week: trust me, it'll add up. If any given week proves too difficult or chaotic, for whatever reason, stick with the same number of minutes for another week. Take a moment to pat yourself on the back for showing up.

6. When you're ready, meaning solid and comfortable in your new habit stack, instead of another minute, add another activity. Then the following week, resume the weekly increase of one minute per practice.

7. Continue the process of gradually adding activities and minutes until you're not merely acclimated to a stack of habits; you feel powerful and delighted with the ongoing progress. You might stop and stabilize at thirty minutes or ninety minutes—it's your call.

The writings of Covey, Ben-Shahar, and Clear sparked my imagination. Having experienced the potency of changing my life one habit at a time, I became determined to show my clients how this work can help create a better life. I put together a series of group workshops dealing with habits and habit stacking. My clients loved it. Many told me it changed their lives. I was on to something. A sense of purpose urged me on. I felt it wasn't enough to share this method with 100 people a month. It needed to be published, so that many more could benefit, including *you*.

A great deal of research has shown that if we repeat an action for twenty-one days, it becomes a habit. Some classic sources want to say thirty days, but let's go with twenty-one—it's less intimidating and therefore more promising. I've recently learned that one can create a new neural pathway in the brain in as few as fourteen days. This is the physiology of forming a habit: neurological events that fire together become wired together. Through repetition, we create ever-stronger neural pathways in our brain and *biologically* increase the likelihood that we will repeat the behavior in the future.

One can create a new neural pathway in the brain in as few as fourteen days. This is the physiology of forming a habit: neurological events that fire together become wired together.

Hanna is a client of mine. She is thirty-four and single, a bit stocky, with a beautiful smile, though sometimes it takes a little patience until it's visible. She complains of being bored, lonely, and sometimes depressed. Hanna decided she could give her mood a boost if she were to choose one thing that would make her home more attractive, since she spends so much time there. It was also less imposing than changing something within herself. So she began her journey to self-improvement by making her bed every morning. She did it for three weeks and then said, "I've got that down. What's next?" Maybe a short stretching routine in her newly neat bedroom would work nicely as the next item in her habit stack. Not being much of an athlete, she searched around on YouTube and found a five-minute set of stretches. And she stuck with it.

The instructor on the YouTube ended the video with a suggestion: "If you have a few more minutes, try this." It was a fifteen-minute strength building workout. Hanna took the bait. After a few weeks, she clicked on a link at the end of *that* video that led her to a fifteen-minute "walking at home" routine. She incorporated that as well. Before long she began to feel foolish indulging in cake or doughnuts at the office after such a nice workout, so she began bringing cut-up fruits or vegetables from home. After a while, she dropped the sugar from her coffee. Next, she substituted green tea with ginger for the coffee. That stimulated her to clean all the fast foods out of her kitchen and join a gym.

Hanna has lost thirty pounds and three dress sizes, is training to compete in a twelve-mile marathon and teaches a Zumba class once a week. Her social life has never been better. She is less moody and more enthusiastic about everything. Our last session was devoted to looking into how she can she find the funds and the tech savvy to produce her own podcast on—you guessed it—habit stacking and self-care.

Not every attempt at personal growth ends up a success story like Hanna's. But habit stacking and baby steps, or as Clear calls them, atomic habits, are realistic approaches to accomplishing your goals.

Think of a small change that will bring you closer to your goals: Going to bed ten minutes earlier. Keeping a clock in the bedroom, so you won't have to risk looking at the phone and getting suckered into scrolling in the middle of the night. Stretching and breathing for five minutes when you're first awake. (More about breathing coming up.) Drinking water or tea when you feel hungry before reaching for the chips. Moving the junk food to a shelf that's harder to reach. Spending five minutes a day focused lovingly on your spouse, looking into each other's eyes. Turning off the phone for fifteen minutes when you pick up the kids. Creating a vision list when you walk into the office.

Here's another habit-making tip. If you want to form a habit, give yourself a visible cue, and make it attractive. Leave your journal on the kitchen table, or put the book you've been wanting to read on your pillow (after you've made the bed). Keep your sneakers next to the bed; watch your favorite sitcom or a cool music video while on the treadmill. Make it easier: couple something you *need* to do with something you *want* to do.

If you want to break a habit, make it invisible. If you spend too much time watching television, move the TV out of the bedroom. If you can't seem to get any work done, put your phone in another room for a few hours and hide the chocolates. Even though you know where they are, making them less accessible gives you more time to pause and notice what it is you *really* want.

The Happiness Advantage

In May 2011, Shawn Achor gave an amazing TED talk titled "The Happiness Advantage: Linking Positive Brains to Performance." It has generated nearly twenty-five million views. I believe its popularity confirms how many of us are feeling a lack of happiness and seeking more. Achor packs well-researched and practical advice into a humorous, highly entertaining twelve-minute talk. You can find it on YouTube.

I've probably watched this talk more than 100 times. I recommend it to all my coaching clients and students. Achor sounds more like a standup comedian than an academic, and his stories and quips stand the test of time. I'll try here to share some of his compelling information without attempting to match his inimitable creative edge.

It's not *objective reality* that defines your experience; rather, the lens through which your brain views the world shapes your reality. If you can change your lens, you can change your experience of happiness.

He cites a number of statistical studies demonstrating that:

- It's not *objective reality* that defines your experience; rather, the lens through which your brain views the world shapes your reality. If you can change your lens, you can change your experience of happiness.
- Through *observing* the external world around you, a mere 10 percent of your happiness is predictable. The other 90 percent is determined by the way your brain *processes* those observations.
- Only 25 percent of success is determined by IQ; 75 percent depends on your degree of optimism, your social support, and your ability to see stress as a challenge rather than a threat.
- In a positive frame of mind, your brain becomes 31 percent more efficient, cultivating what Achor calls the "Happiness Advantage." Intelligence, creativity, and energy levels all rise.

The mood-altering hormone dopamine not only makes you happier, but it also activates all the learning centers in the brain.

To put these principles into practice, Achor promotes a five-point, twenty-one-day program for achieving lasting positive change, culled from several sources in the expanding world of positive psychology. Every day for three weeks:

- Write down three new things for which you are grateful.
- Journal about one positive experience that occurred during that day. By writing it down, we relive it.
- Exercise for ten minutes.
- Meditate for eight to ten minutes. This allows the brain to override the culturally induced ADHD of modern life.
- Perform random acts of kindness. These can be as simple as texting a kind message to a colleague or a friend.

2

A Meditation Memoir

In 1967 we were living in Eldorado Springs, Colorado, at the end of a winding, mountainous road. We were among the first hippies in the Boulder area, and certainly the only married longhairs in town. We spent a lot of time sitting in a circle with friends, passing around a sugar bowl filled with hot peppermint tea and honey, blissfully high and listening to this revolutionary new album by the Beatles called *Sergeant Pepper's Lonely Hearts Club Band*. We loved that sugar bowl, because it had two handles, making it easier to pass and hence more emblematic of our communal life. We shared our thoughts as fluently as our tea. One of us mentioned that the glorious Beatles were heading to India to learn Transcendental Meditation (TM) with a guru named Maharishi Mahesh Yogi. It didn't take us long to discover that a TM center had opened in Manhattan, initiating would-be meditators a bit more locally than at his ashram (that is, in the Western Hemisphere).

After two weeks of complete sobriety, as prescribed by the guru, we flew East to study the method. The initiation ceremony took place in an upscale Lexington Avenue brownstone, and it involved each individual bringing an offering of flowers, fruit, rice, and incense to a picture of Maharishi's master, Guru Dev. Somehow it seemed perfectly normal at the time; looking back now, I wonder how we accepted that ceremony so uncritically. Our guide was Prudence Farrow, known to some as Mia's sister, but to us she was "Dear Prudence" from the Beatles' fabulous *White Album*.

We were taught to meditate twice a day for twenty to thirty minutes, silently repeating to ourselves a mantra that had been given us. When the mind would wander, as it inevitably did, we were taught to gently turn our attention back to the mantra. We were assured that after five to eight years of practice, we would achieve God consciousness, or at the very least cosmic consciousness. We weren't sure exactly what that would look like, but it sounded good.

That was the beginning of what has now become fifty-five years of practicing meditation and mindfulness. Before long we outgrew Maharishi and his commercialized approach to Hindu meditation, but the desire to cultivate a peaceful spirit in a maddening world remained.

Our research led us to the work of Dr. Herbert Benson. Benson was an American cardiologist, professor of mind/body medicine at Harvard Medical School, and founder of the Benson-Henry Institute for Mind Body Medicine at Massachusetts General Hospital. He astutely captured the essence of the TM methodology and divested it of its mystical flavor and cultural origins. He named this reconstituted technique The *Relaxation Response*.

Eliciting the relaxation response is simple, Benson explained: once or twice daily, for ten to twenty minutes, sit in a relaxed position with eyes closed and mentally repeat a word or sound as you breathe easily and naturally. Some people choose to use a word with a specifically comforting meaning, such as "love" or "peace." Others say a word or phrase drawn from their familiar traditional prayers. Dr. Benson suggests taking the word "one" as the vehicle for achieving the relaxation response, since it is so simple and comfortable that it will facilitate ease and a lack of distraction. As with other forms of meditation, if one's thoughts should stray, which is normal and expected, one simply allows the mind to refocus on the silent internal expression of the word. Yet it's not actually repetitious at all; in fact, every moment spent in meditation has the capacity to free us from repetitive, mindless patterns of thought and help us tap into new levels of inner experience.

I like to think of meditation as a way of doing nothing that affects everything. Meditating in the morning adds clarity to your thought process, weeds out a lot of emotionally tinged rumination and monkey-brain thinking, and produces calm. In the words of Deepak Chopra, a one-time disciple of Maharishi who went on to establish his own popular path and write extensively, "Meditation is not a way of making the mind quiet. It is a way to enter the quiet that is already there."

I like to think of meditation as a way of doing nothing that affects everything.

Studies have shown that meditation promotes neurogenesis, the formation of new neurons in the brain—once considered controversial in adult humans, but more widely understood in recent years. Neurons (also called neurones or nerve cells) are the fundamental units of the brain and nervous system, the cells responsible for receiving sensory input from the external world, sending motor commands to our muscles, and transforming and relaying electrical signals at every step in between. Their interactions define who we are as people and how we react to external stimuli and decode new information. Neural pathways are the patterns defined by the ways in which your mind tends to travel, well-paved routes through the complex network of neurons. These pathways represent what we commonly experience as habits.

Until recently it was believed that the adult brain deteriorates over time and is incapable of regenerating new neurons. In the 1990s this was disproven, as evidence began to emerge that meditation can be an antidote to such diseases as dementia and Alzheimer's. Today meditation and exercise have been tagged as key components in an effective anti-aging system, and have been shown to reduce anxiety and depression, lower blood pressure, and increase immunity. As Jessica Cassity, author and *New York Times* journalist, observes:

With meditation, your brain is effectively being rewired. As your feelings and thoughts morph toward a more pleasant outlook, your brain is also transforming, making this way of thought more of a default. . . . The more your brain changes from meditation, the more you react to everyday life with that same sense of calm, compassion, and awareness.

Calm, compassionate, aware. The more mindful we become, the more we meditate, the more the brain adapts to these new, improved sensibilities as our default state. This is why meditation has such a big impact on those who meditate, even beyond their dedicated practice time: they have taught their brains to be mindful, tranquil, at peace, and centered all throughout the day—not just when actively meditating. The regular practice of meditation is one of the most potent rituals we can embrace in our daily lives to acquire the constant mental, emotional, and physical well-being we all crave. And it can be done without the formal trappings of religious ritual.

3

Of Breathwork, Yogis, and Coaches

The year is 1970. We are living in the foothills of the Rockies in our first real home. It is a painted Victorian lady, with olive green clapboards and canary yellow shutters with electric blue cornflowers stenciled on the trim. The house was lovingly painted by a group of devotees from the Krishna Temple in exchange for several 100-pound bags of brown rice and other plant-based staples. The living room is a warm apricot (the color of the guru's robes), with Indian bedspreads draped from the ceiling, and the dining room is lavender with a long homemade oak table close to the floor. The scent of sandalwood incense saturates every room, particularly the dining room. Spiritual seekers sit on embroidered stuffed rice sacks in cross-legged position at my vegetarian cooking classes, eating macrobiotic delicacies with chopsticks. And yes, the bronze bell is in the middle of the table, flanked by tamari (naturally fermented soy sauce) and gomasio (roasted sesame seeds and sea salt, ground with a mortar and pestle).

Boulder is about to host its first major spiritual festival, and as leaders in the community we have been asked to host one of the celebrated guests. We were given the choice of Yogi Bhajan or Rabbi Shlomo Carlebach. Unable to imagine what we would have in common with a bearded rabbi, we chose the yogi. He was a towering figure, no less than six feet four, and a former Mr. India. His diet consisted of watermelon and rice cakes toasted with butter and garlic, soaked almonds, and sautèed vegetables. I couldn't understand how anyone could get so big and strong eating like that, but my neighbors on the Plains were bison who grazed on wild wheat, so why not?

Yogi taught me two important lessons. The first was about raising my child. My New Age Hebrew cowboy, Adam, was a toddler, and he ruled the house with an iron fist. He had never heard the word no. Even if he would, it would hardly dissuade him. Yogi taught me that Adam needed rules, boundaries, discipline. In the gentle spirit of ahimsa—compassionate nonviolence—he explained to me that if a child grows up thinking it's OK to have an "f-you" attitude toward his mother, he will eventually say "f-you" to God. I was shocked! The sentence still rings in my ears. It would be years before I could apply that sort of discipline and boundaries to my own parenting style.

The second lesson was about raising my consciousness through my breath. Every night at 3:30 a.m. Yogi would wake up the house to assemble in the apricot room. This hour of pre-dawn quietude, known as the Brahma Muhurta, is believed to be ideal for spiritual activities, meditation, yoga, and prayers. It is considered the most conducive time for connecting with higher consciousness, inner reflection, and focusing the mind. The peacefulness and stillness of the early morning hours are thought to support deeper spiritual practices.

According to Hindu belief, during the Brahma Muhurta the world is said to be at its purest and calmest state. The environment is thought to be free from distractions, and the mind is considered more receptive and focused, making it easier to attain spiritual progress. We sang and chanted, usually culminating in one of three particularly effective breathing, or pranayama, exercises. One was a well-known method of alternate nostril breathing called *nadi suddhi*. Another was what Yogi Bhajan called "happy breaths," which incorporated vigorous circular movements of the arms and a wonderful, intentional smile that could not help but gladden the heart with every exhale.

The third was called the Breath of Fire. It often resulted in some serious hyperventilation. Breath of Fire is comprised of short, rapid inhalations and exhalations, invariably leading to a surge of energy. Many of us felt more awake, alert, and revitalized after practicing this (even at 3:30 a.m.). Some experienced a natural high, with increased mental clarity and heightened awareness. The rhythmic breathing pattern focuses the mind and improves concentration. Improbably, it also induces a sense of relaxation. It calms the mind and reduces stress or anxiety. Many participants felt a sense of internal cleansing or purification after practicing Breath of Fire. It is believed to help the body release toxins, generating a sensation of warmth or tingling in the body, particularly in the abdominal region, where the breath is focused.

While our responses varied, everyone agreed that conscious breathing is a powerful tool. Interestingly, in Hebrew the word for *breath* is *neshima,* and the word for *soul* is *neshama.* They are spelled the same except for a different vowel marking under the second syllable.

Once Yogi left our home, the 3:30 sessions came to an end, but the breathwork we had learned became part of my life. I now frequently begin and end my daily meditation practice with conscious breathing, a few minutes of simply inhaling deeply, bringing the air into the stomach, and then to the lungs. These inhalations are followed by long, gentle exhalations, feeling the belly drop and relaxing with each breath. Sometimes I add a body scan, paying effortless attention first to the toes, and then to the subtle energy rising up to the head, relaxing each area as I exhale.

The Three Breaths Meditation

I have a few favorite breathing exercises, each one tailored to a specific need. The Three Breaths Meditation is a great first step for becoming more present, more mindful. Mindfulness has become a buzzword these days, and rightfully so. Never before has a generation been so not-present-in-the-moment as ours. Can we stop worrying that we are already late for something that hasn't happened yet?

When we release the baggage of the past and the anxiety that clouds the future, the *now* becomes alive and colorful. In *flow,* we are fully immersed in what we're doing, consciously aware, productive, nonstop, eyes open, alert, and grounded. Here's how you do the Three Breaths, seated comfortably on a chair:

When we release the baggage of the past and the anxiety that clouds the future, the *now* becomes alive and colorful. In *flow*, we are fully immersed in what we're doing, consciously aware.

With your first breath, inhale deeply and gently. As you inhale, feel the energy flow all the way down to your feet on the ground, and to your bottom on the chair where you sit. As you exhale, let go of any and all regrets. The past is the past, and you've done the best you could.

With the next breath, inhale deeply again; be aware of the way the energy of the air fills your lungs and all your organs, and of how the newly refreshed organs faithfully nourish you from within. As you exhale, let go of any worries about the future—even tomorrow, even ten minutes from now. What is about to happen is an open book. Why let the unknown and the unknowable sap your energy, your focus, your joy?

With the third breath, inhale deeply, and feel your connection to all the goodness you have shared with the world, to the beautiful person you are inside, and to the powerful, positive potential that resides within. As you exhale, come fully present into the Now, with gratitude, focus, clarity, and calm.

Claim your *flow*!

Breathwork is a fundamental aspect of many ancient cultures and spiritual traditions. Practices like pranayama in yoga, Taoist breathing techniques, and various forms of meditation centered on following the breath have long incorporated breath control for physical, mental, and spiritual purposes. Age-old healing systems, such as Traditional Chinese Medicine and Ayurveda, also emphasize the importance of breath in maintaining health and balance within the body.

The New Age movement of the 1960s and '70s helped revive interest in ancient spiritual practices, including breathwork, as people sought alternative approaches to health and spirituality. Today breathwork is touted for its ability to lower anxiety, deal with trauma, heal illness by increasing oxygenation, improve mental clarity, and regulate emotions. Since about 2020, breathwork training has gone viral on the Internet. Many coaches are adopting it as part of their practice, and dedicated breathwork sessions are popping up everywhere.

Numerous scientific studies at Cambridge University and other highly respected research centers are exploring the potential benefits of breathwork and its integration into holistic wellness approaches. The modern scientific jury is still out about its effectiveness, but in terms of achieving calm and improving focus, I can tell you that it is enormously helpful.

Adopt a few simple breathing exercises as a part of your habit stack. Adding a few moments of mindful breathing to your day will enhance your physical well-being and your ability to feel more connected and whole. If you are the sort of person who implements new habits better in a group setting, find a breathwork session in your neighborhood. For most of us, one or two sessions will suffice to find a style that is best for you.

If you are looking at breathwork as a supplement to therapy or as a replacement for psychotropic drugs, I applaud you. Before engaging in breathwork practices, however, it is important to practice under guidance, especially with the more intense techniques, and to consider your individual health condition. before engaging in breathwork practices. I have worked with a number of trainers and practitioners and will say unequivocally that it will prove worth your while to try.

4

The Journal Unbound

*I don't journal to "be productive." I don't do it to find
great ideas or to put down prose I can later publish.
The pages aren't intended for anyone but me. It's the
most cost-effective therapy I've ever found.*

—Tim Ferris

When it comes to rituals, perhaps the most dynamic change in my emotional well-being has come about through journaling. I started this practice during a tumultuous period, while in the throes of a divorce. I was brimming over with unpleasant emotions: anger, sadness, hopelessness, and a sense of victimhood. I felt it was all too dark to share with anyone but my therapist, and one hour a week could hardly cover it. "If I can't find a constructive way to release all that pain and anger," I thought, "I'll surely explode."

I embraced journaling as a key to coaching myself, and I feel confident passing this key on to you for your own adventures in self-coaching.

I bought a red college lined spiral notebook (red for blood? for rage?) and began my journey. Today I look over those tormented pages and wonder how I managed to survive. My journal was like a release valve that let out just enough pressure to keep me from bursting. I learned that journaling allows for healthy emotional growth and helps us make sense of all the negative, confounding thoughts that tumble around in our aching brains.

My journaling practice has become as normal a part of my daily routine as breakfast or a shower. Call me a fanatic, but there are notebooks strewn about in nearly every corner of my home—brightly colored, college-lined, easy to find; smaller, unlined journals covered in plush purple velvet; little black Moleskins that fit in my purse; fancy Day-Timers that came with a guarantee that they'll organize my life. (Ha!) Some pages record feelings of gratitude from day to day, or a great quote that triggered a new idea. Some are more lyrical: impressions of a magical moment on a mountain in Colorado or an orchid garden in Singapore. Others are mostly incoherent morning pages, daily stream-of-consciousness blurts, designed to open the mind and heart, and bulldoze creative blocks. (More about that a bit later.)

I began coaching professionally in the 1990s. Because I experienced great strides with my own personal practice of journaling, it soon became an integral part of my work with clients as well, helping them discover their own pathways to personal transformation. Journaling has helped my clients deepen self-knowledge and mindful awareness and nourish a sustained sense of well-being. Journaling helps us acquire the skills and sensibilities that lead to a more positive, focused, and productive life.

The average person thinks about 75,000 thoughts a day, but usually articulates fewer than 10 percent of those. Even the most enthusiastic journaler probably doesn't set down more than 1 percent of those verbalized thoughts. Speaking can be a wonderfully effective mode of communication with others. Writing, however, is the introspective art of cultivating, refining, and unleashing the true potency of thought. Spoken words vanish quickly into the vast universe; the written word stands forever—substantiated, reified, real. Through journaling, thoughts become palpable, visions come to life, once-dull days become permeated with fullness of mind. In the words of American author Flannery O'Connor: "I write because I don't know what I think until I read what I say."

Many of the great minds of history kept a journal: Isaac Newton, Abraham Lincoln, Leonardo da Vinci, Charles Darwin, Winston Churchill, Menachem Mendel Schneerson, Benjamin Franklin, Ernest Hemingway, George Bernard Shaw, Stephen Covey, Queen Victoria, and Maya Angelou, to name a few. It would be an exaggeration to ascribe their successes to their journaling, but thinking through writing must have been a powerful tool in the clarification of their thought. Journaling helped them prioritize and refine their thinking and thereby fulfill their most cherished dreams and goals. There's virtually no limit to what journaling can do for you.

Over the years I've disposed of pages and pages of extraneous to-do lists, obsolete landline numbers, and reminders about those obscure items I imagined I couldn't live without and will probably never buy. But I'll never let the notebooks go. They are my history, the roadmap of my soul.

I'll never let the notebooks go. They are my history, the roadmap of my soul.

Commit to keeping a journal for a month. Start small and simple. Take baby steps—atomic habits—because when we get overly ambitious, we're more likely to give up early in the game. Anchor your journaling to something that is already a well-established habit, like your morning coffee, or "I always take ten minutes to journal after I run." Keep your notebook in a convenient and visible place, with a pen right next to it so you don't have any excuses.

Next, become accountable. Let your friends or your spouse know you are journaling every day. Make it part of your identity. Refer to yourself as a journaler. Reward yourself at the end of the month for a job well done. Your journal will be a reward in and of itself, but if not, perhaps a kayak rental or a thick slice of dulce de leche cheesecake at your favorite restaurant will be enticing enough to motivate you.

There are many ways to journal. I'd like to share a few that I prescribe to my clients. Try them and see which of them speak to you. As self-help guru Tim Ferris said, the pages aren't for anyone but you. These tools will help you to deepen your knowledge of who you are; to celebrate small victories that you might not otherwise have noticed; to upgrade your positivity quotient; to identify what you really need to be more productive, focused, and nourished. Sounds good? Find a comfortable chair, a notebook that appeals, a favorite pen, and let 'er rip!

All beginnings are difficult. But begin writing no matter what. As the prolific American novelist Louis L'Amour said, "The water does not flow until the faucet is turned on." Your words, permanently etched on paper, turn into your legacy, your guideposts, the barometer of who you truly are and what you really need.

Your Daily VeGGGies

When I turned twelve, I received a shimmering pink diary with a tiny lock and key as a birthday present. On its pastel pages, I scribbled my dreams, my fears, and the names of the boys who had stepped on my feet when we were slow dancing. I kept it in my underwear drawer and stealthily retrieved it in late evenings when the house was quiet. I remember editing it at times, concerned that someone was bound to find it if I died. (That same motivation inspired me to bring my Reese's Peanut Butter Cup wrappers to the kitchen trashcan rather than disposing of them in my room.) It was a start.

VeGGGies were my next attempt. This method is a lot more specific (not to mention more sophisticated) than a teenager's secret diary, but both can basically be seen as variations on the journaling theme. *VeGGGies* is an acronym for one personal *Victory* and three things I am *Grateful* for each day. I learned this technique from my friend and teacher Dr. Miriam Adahan, a gifted therapist and prolific writer, who is a master of emotional intelligence. Dr. Adahan is especially known for using a wide variety of approaches to helping her clients avoid psychiatric medication whenever possible. Her courses on emotional maturity, and my sharing of her methods among groups of friends, constituted my first formal venture into coaching some thirty-five years ago.

Activating the RAS

One theory about the benefits of writing down our "gratitudes" centers on a network of neurons in our brains known as the reticular activating system, or RAS. Among other functions, the RAS is the reason why, when you learn a new word, you suddenly start hearing it everywhere. The RAS takes what you focus on and creates a filter for it, sifting through the data and presenting only the pieces that are significant to you. The RAS seeks information that confirms your beliefs. It helps you to see what you want to see. Focus on the bad, and your dark thoughts will invite negativity into your life. Focus on the good things, and you will find a wealth of information that supports your upbeat outlook. Good things will come to you precisely because your brain is searching for them. The RAS offers a biological and neurological explanation of a long-standing spiritual phenomenon that has become known in recent times as the *law of attraction*. Think well, and life will be better!

Years ago, I began writing down three things I was grateful for each day. It was 1998, and my life was wretched. My marriage was falling apart. My peaceful home felt like a city in the Ukraine that was being pummeled out of nowhere by bombs. My teenage kids were responding to the tension by acting out in school. My bank account was dwindling, and so were my hopes. To say it in the most delicate of terms, I was screwed. But over the course of time, my gratitude notebook effectively cleansed my lenses so that I could see the potential for good in all my traumas and reframe tough circumstances as opportunities.

You don't need to write full sentences. Bullet points will work just fine. The essential action here is identifying the things, people, moments, and unexpected openings you are grateful for, and taking the time to write them down. Once you start looking for three, you will find many more, and they'll become increasingly meaningful. When we appreciate the good things, good things appreciate.

Personal victories are the second phase of this exercise. We tend to downplay our successes and concentrate on our shortcomings and failures. The reason is simple enough: when things are going well, they just go, without drama or fanfare. When we mess up, we lunge into fight-or-flight mode, producing prodigious amounts of adrenaline. This causes our heart rate to accelerate, our breathing to become shallow, and our fists to clench. The body is signaling us that something terribly important is happening, and we underscore those negative moments. They stand out like highlighted paragraphs on a page. The many positive moments in our lives might easily go unnoticed if we don't take the time to write them down. Remember who really owns that yellow highlighter: *you*.

In keeping with the idea of taking baby steps—atomic changes—and James Clear's 1 percent rule, it's easy to see why small victories are worthy of celebration. Documenting these seemingly insignificant positive accomplishments will bring you closer to being the person you want to be. Establishing good habits and making better choices isn't just about filling your days with clever life hacks that produce healthier teeth, shinier hair, cleaner closets, or other external measures of success. It's the small, sustainable victories that will eventually effect the greatest change.

Journaling as Therapy: Expressive Writing

While my focus in this book is to encourage readers to coach themselves, I am always hesitant to suggest that anyone try to be her own therapist. We all have unresolved issues and small-T traumas in our personal histories that can affect the quality of our lives. Some are more manageable than others. There are times when our moods or behaviors might call for professional therapeutic attention. If your thoughts or emotions or behavior are out of control—especially if they're affecting your relationships, your work, or your sense of well-being—it's time for help. But in less critical situations, our self-coaching skills will suffice.

There's a particularly effective form of journaling known as *expressive writing*. It can be a fabulous process for bringing comfort and healing to those dark, sad places within. James W. Pennebaker is an American social scientist and professor of psychology at the University of Texas. His innovative research demonstrates that people who have experienced trauma and keep it hidden—from others, from themselves, or both—are those most likely to have health issues. To address what he saw as this statistical reality, he developed the exercise known as *expressive writing*. He found it to be a practice that can improve moods, lower anxiety, strengthen the immune system, lower blood pressure, and promote healthy choices. He has published several books on the subject. I recommend *Opening Up by Writing It Down: How Expressive Writing Improves Health and Eases Emotional Pain*. But if, like many of us, you're hard-pressed to find the time or the motivation to read yet another book, here's an abridged version of Dr. Pennebaker's method:

Over a period of three to four days, resolve to write about a deep emotional challenge that has had an impact on your life. Allow yourself to really let go and think about the event and the ways it has affected you. It may have been a childhood experience, an unresolved issue in a relationship with a loved one, or something related to your work.

- Find a quiet time and place where you won't be disturbed.
- Write continuously for twenty minutes.
- Don't think about grammar or spelling.
- Write about something important and personal.
- Don't chose a trauma that is so recent and overwhelming that it is still keeping you off-balance.
- Write only for yourself, without concern for what others may say.

If after three or four days of writing, you want to take the process further and deeper, use your imagination and think about writing on the subject from the perspectives of other people who were involved in a similar situation.

From time to time I read through the journals I kept while going through my divorce or handling the mental health issues of my daughter. Those were the darkest days of my life; yet I had to go on as a mother of young children and as an educator, showing up with a smile on my face, putting dinner on the table, and devising new and interesting lessons for my classes. I am convinced that the time I spent journaling—naming, facing, and disclosing the fear, anger, and sadness I was experiencing in these moments—helped me stay sane and strong.

Good Morning, Me!

Writing is medicine. It is an appropriate antidote to injury.
It is an appropriate companion for any difficult change.

—JULIA CAMERON

There's another marvelous form of journaling that is not so much about addressing emotional challenges as unleashing the creativity within to liberate your muse. It's explained in wonderful detail in Julia Cameron's book *The Artist's Way*. It's not just for artists; it's a practical guide to getting in touch with your own internal voice, a way of becoming your own closest friend. As such, it becomes a springboard for unblocking the giving of your gift—be it in writing, creating music, some other expression of your talents, or simply in communicating freely and openly with the people who share your world. There are workshops available on the Internet or in your community that can help you get started. Or you can explore *The Artist's Way* on your own. There is a companion workbook, filled with perceptive writing prompts, that can effectively help you to connect with her method.

Cameron's program consists primarily of introducing two practices into your life—one daily, and one weekly. The daily practice is called "morning pages." Immediately upon rising in the morning, take pen to paper and write three pages of longhand, stream-of-consciousness, unfiltered monologue. The pages aren't meant to be planned, edited, or even reread; they're a means of siphoning off the mind's surface noise and achieving flow so that you can access and exercise your deeper thoughts and impulses, not just then and there but subsequently throughout the day. Cameron describes morning pages as "metabolizing life." Sometimes the process helps to work through intense rites of passage such as death, a love affair, or the loss of a friend, often indirectly rather than head-on. In more upbeat circumstances, the pages can act as a muse or a cheerleader, spurring you on to dream new dreams or enthusiastically take that next step. The cumulative effect of daily morning pages is extraordinary. You grow more intimate with yourself and as a result more intimately engaged with the world beyond.

The weekly practice is the "artist's date"—a solitary excursion to a location that has the potential to inspire or excite you or pique your creative interest in something new. It could be a thrift shop, museum, bookstore, botanical garden, or some unfamiliar ethnic culinary outlet. Cameron notes that while morning pages are work, the artist's date is play—which ironically can make it more challenging for many of us. Playfulness, whimsy, imagination, even mischief, are among the characteristics of youth that we might be wise to reclaim as adults.

I love artist's dates, because I can justify meandering with no sense of direction, window shopping, or tripping out in Home Depot on a random Tuesday in November. I'm just drinking in stimuli that will swirl around in my brain until I put together the pieces of a puzzle that I didn't even know was there.

5

What Are Your Strengths?

As an educator, a coach, and a mother of seven, I have observed this time and time again: whenever I catch someone doing something well and say it out loud, the positivity spills over into the rest of their performance. If, on the other hand, I point out a weakness, it puts a damper on their strengths. I've discovered a worthwhile exercise called Reflected Best Self (RBS) that helps us to tap into our talents.

To begin with, start gathering input from family, friends, colleagues, and teachers. Ask what they see as your key strengths. Search for common themes in their feedback to develop a clearer picture. Next, write a description of yourself that summarizes and distills the accumulated information. Finally, having discovered or rediscovered what you're best at, build on that and redesign your understanding of your ideal life. Once you're more aware of your character strengths, you can shape the roles you choose to play.

Character strengths are the positive parts of your person-ality that make you feel authentic and engaged. When you discover your greatest qualities, you can use them to build your best life. Strength building has been shown to boost confidence, which in turn helps you to accomplish your goals. Your goals become clearer, because they are consistent with your strengths. This will certainly make you happier and reduce a lot of stress in your life. I often use the ridiculous metaphor of an elephant who tries to act like a butterfly. It's hopeless—even Dumbo couldn't pull it off for long.

More specifically (and plausibly), it's a rare baseball player who is equally good at every position. Why should a natural pitcher strive to develop his skills as a right fielder? The better alternative is to foster excellence in the budding pitcher by identifying and harnessing his unique strengths.

It is a paradox of human psychology that while people *remember* criticism, they *respond* to praise. The former renders them defensive and therefore unlikely to change, while the latter produces confidence and the desire to improve performance.

When I was the principal of a private high school, the dean of the school became my inspirational mentor. He had developed a relationship with a personal life coach before anyone knew what that meant, and he communicated with a Blackberry when the rest of us still thought it was a fruit that grew on a low-lying bush. He also happened to be a drop-dead gorgeous British rugby player, and charismatic to boot. He encouraged us all to grow, both as a collaborative admin team and as individuals. We had professional retreats and played team building games.

The most valuable exercise for me was strength finding. We did the survey referred to above as an RBS; I also took a fifteen-minute survey from VIA Institute on Character that defined my top 5 strengths. For me it was a life changer. My top five strengths were love, spirituality, perspective, appreciation of beauty and excellence, and social intelligence. Once I realized that my gifts were communication, teambuilding, and coaching my staff to reach their potential, I started spending more and more of my time at work doing just that. I became an educational coach and took seminars at Harvard as well as a remarkable training in Boulder, Colorado, called Passageways. I took the lead for the entire school in formulating and implementing professional development as well as troubleshooting interpersonal issues between teachers, students, administration, and staff. I also got better at delegating—for example, empowering my guidance counselor to design a rubric for report card comments. Tasks that were technical or that called for strictly linear thinking became less relevant in my life, and I ceased beating myself up for not tackling them. I was not a technical administrator, but a people person, and I played it to the hilt, with terrific results.

Suddenly I became intoxicated with my job; it became not a job, but a calling. I couldn't wait to get to school in the morning. In short, I followed the core strategy of strengths training, playing up my strengths rather than being overly concerned about my weaknesses. It worked like a charm. And it made perfect sense: how much can you tell me about Kobe Bryant, besides basketball? Or about Fred Astaire, other than dance? Or Pavarotti, aside from song? Each one pursued the perfection of a talent he already excelled at and became a superstar.

How much can you tell me about Kobe Bryant, besides basketball? Or about Fred Astaire, other than dance? Or Pavarotti, aside from song? Each one pursued the perfection of a talent he already excelled at and became a superstar.

You don't necessarily need a formal relationship with a coach to develop the habit of focusing on and underscoring your strengths. This mindset can be cultivated, one imaginary yellow highlight at a time, along with a mental delete key with which to dump all that sabotaging self-talk about your weaknesses.

6

Posttraumatic Growth

But what about our weaknesses? What can we do about those traumatic moments that can make a person feel like a failure, a misfit, maybe even in such deep despair that it feels like having fallen into a pit from which there is no escape?

Or maybe it isn't so much about you. It may be the terrors of a world gone wrong, or events that make no sense, that have thrown you off your game. It could have been a violent invasion of your once-secure world, or the inexplicable sudden death of a loved one. An accident, a fire.

PTSD (posttraumatic stress disorder) has become a ubiquitous acronym in our society. We all have friends or family members who have been so scarred by trauma that posttraumatic stress appears all but inevitable. One needn't look very far to find researchers, authors, spiritual leaders, and healers who are addressing trauma in their work. But how many of us are familiar with *posttraumatic growth?* Perhaps we can become smarter, go deeper, and become more open and adventurous because of the very trauma that seems so insurmountable. Trauma can become a gift.

Let's call it resilience. To understand resilience, picture yourself holding one of those pink high-bouncer balls, the kind kids used to play "A—my name is Alice, and I live in Alabama . . . B—my name is Betty, and I live in Baltimore." Or, in an earlier era, the ball that boys used to play stickball and sent flying for a city block. Now imagine you're smashing that high-bouncer down onto the concrete with all your strength. You know what happens next. It'll bounce back very high, higher than the height from which you cast it down. That's resilience. Posttraumatic growth is not denying the pain and distress caused by trauma; it emphasizes the potential for positive change in its aftermath. When some trauma throws us to the ground, we can bounce back still higher—if we have the right moves in place.

Here's what I often suggest to my clients:

- We must know that it is possible to grow. If we feel that our present state can't change, it won't.
- We must give ourselves permission to be human. It might take some tears to allow our unhappiness or fear to express itself. Whether by talking it through or journaling our way over the roadblocks, it'll take some time.
- We need to create recovery time. Every two hours, take five minutes off. Do the breathing exercise given in chapter 3, or some other soothing meditation. Listen to music you love. Be sure to get seven to eight hours of sleep each night. Time off is a must. Take one day off

every week. Take one month off every year. The famous American business tycoon J. P. Morgan said, "I can do the work of a year in nine months, but not in twelve."

- Maintain a gratitude practice. Gratitude and happiness are inextricably intertwined.

- Increase acts of kindness. When we transform from helpless to helpful, we also morph from hopeless to hopeful.

- Find three things you can look forward to in the future. Positively anticipating the future can greatly contribute to your resilience for several reasons. Looking forward to the future often involves setting goals or having a sense of purpose. When we have something to strive for, it can provide the direction and motivation that helps us navigate more effectively through challenges and over obstacles. Take a moment to write three things to which you're looking forward.

When some trauma throws us to the ground, we can bounce back still higher—if we have the right moves in place.

A positive view of the future fosters hope, optimism, and trust—not just *despite* past traumas, but *because of* them—and having bounced back. Believing that there are better times ahead, even in the face of adversity, often acts as a buffer against the stresses of difficult situations. Looking ahead can also create a psychological distance from difficulties in the present.

This shift in perspective can reduce the perceived impact of current hardships, making them seem only temporary, and therefore more manageable. Overall, looking forward to the future empowers us to adopt a proactive stance towards challenges, fostering a sense of agency and capability, contributing significantly to our resilience in facing adversity.

7

Worrying

We all tend to worry—about the world, about our families, about our health, about our investments. We entertain worst-case scenarios, engage in a lot of negative future-tripping, allow our anxieties to overtake us. Yes, in many cases there is valid cause for concern, but too much worry can lead to chronic, debilitating anxiety. Research has shown that anxiety can disturb your sleep, tax your immune system, raise the risk of post-traumatic stress disorder and other mental health issues, and even shorten your life.

Yet most chronic worriers have mixed feelings about their worries. There can in fact be an upside to worrying. When we have genuine issues to deal with, it makes sense to worry. We need to be ready for anything: "I have to be responsible." Or "Denial doesn't make problems disappear." This can get a little slippery. For example, we often confuse worrying with planning. A worrier might convince himself that obsessing over every potentially disastrous contingency and exploring all the pitfalls will head off an otherwise inevitable disaster. It can be difficult to let go of worry when it seems as though your worries have been effective.

Notice whether you've been revisiting the same issue again and again. Are you making progress, such as in handling the anxiety by writing down concrete, detailed plans, and acting on them? Or does it feel like a broken record, helplessly ruminating, running in frenzied mental and emotional circles like a hamster on a wheel?

Even if you were to decide that you simply must stop agonizing over every negative eventuality, it's usually not so simple. The effort is likely to have the opposite effect. So don't try to "just say no."

Worry Time and the Art of Letting Go

Instead, you might create a space for worrying in your day. Pick a time and a place, preferably the same time and place, every day. During the rest of the day, whenever anxieties come to mind, just jot them down and postpone them until it's "worry time." When the time arrives, go over your list of things to worry about. Decide which are real, which are unlikely, and which are utterly imaginary. If it's real, it's most likely solvable. Take some time to brainstorm several solutions to the problem. If possible, take an extra moment to write down logical solutions and next steps, and when worry time is over, move on. You may think you don't have time for this, but ruminating for hours while you are supposed to be present for other activities can hijack your entire life. By allowing yourself to postpone your worrying rather than trying to stop it, you are gaining control over your thoughts. Postponing your worry is effective because you are not suppressing it; you're simply saying, "I am not worrying about this now." Over time, you will come to be amazed at how much command you have over your once-compulsive emotional tone.

By allowing yourself to postpone your worrying rather than trying to stop it, you are gaining control over your thoughts.

In a 2010 study, scientists from Harvard University investigated how mind wandering affects happiness. They created a smartphone app that periodically asked a few thousand participants how happy they were feeling, what were they doing, and whether their thoughts were focused on the current activity or worrying about something else.

The researchers found that people spend almost half of their time thinking about something unconnected to their current task and that they were less happy during those moments. Moreover, positive thoughts had little effect on their mood, whereas neutral and negative thoughts made them considerably less happy. The research ascertained that a wandering mind affects happiness more than any activity.

These results suggest that recurrent worries are detrimental to our state of well-being, overtake our pleasant moments, and rob us of our joy. Further studies at universities in the United Kingdom indicate that multitasking has adverse effects on IQ as well as on brain density in the areas responsible for empathy and emotional control.

In addition to establishing a worry time, it would be a good idea to avail ourselves of a "letting go time," specifically with regard to anxiety. Here we can adapt and repurpose some of the exercises I've mentioned earlier, such as the Three Breaths Meditation. The more specific the focus on an anxiety-producing train of thought, the more effective will the three breaths method be.

"Letting go of the past and all its troubles" and "letting go of the future and all its worries" are a bit abstract and slippery for most of us to wrap our brains around. (Let alone our stubborn nervous systems.) Give those exhalations from deep within something real and resonant to release. Be specific and true to your real feelings; don't scrimp on the details. When it comes to the third exhalation, you'll be equipped to arrive fully present in a moment of tangible growth, past the pain of a moment ago, to a peaceful and positive shift, going forward in moments and days to come.

You can practice this periodically throughout the day, not just at worry time. You can link such techniques to transitions, like getting into the car, or starting a new activity, such as sitting down to the computer or preparing a meal—wherever and whenever you can find a minute that is comfortable enough to honestly turn your attention inside.

Sometimes I'll make a list of the things that are worrying me I fold a paper into three columns and label them: "My Basket," "God's Basket," and "Someone Else's Basket." If the item lands in My Basket, I jot down one or two possible solutions. If it lands in God's Basket or Someone Else's Basket, I'll cross it out while still allowing it to be legible—so I can remind myself in the future not to waste time and energy trying to handle it alone, but to keep my eyes open as the solution unfolds.

Guided visualization can also be tailored to the task of letting go of anxiety. Imagine your worries like clouds in the sky. Watch them gently pass and observe as new clouds arrive. The clouds come and go; some of them may look threatening; but they too shall pass, and you are still you. You understand the benefits and practice the art of positive thinking, so when you see your thoughts turning gray and gloomy, you can gently escort them to a sunnier place. If you've ever done a simple stretching exercise and felt the sudden release of muscular tension, you know how sweet it can be. With practice, it can become almost as easy and automatic to let go of stress as it is to become tense in the first place.

8

The Toolbox

In this chapter, I'm going to present an array of tools that will help you manage your life and emotions more easily and successfully.

Nondominant Handwriting

Are you right-handed or left-handed? Never mind, no matter. Righty or lefty, when you write with your other, nondominant hand, you activate areas of the brain that normally lie dormant, so you can access territory beyond the limitations of rational, linear thought.

This extraordinary exercise is performed with the left hand if you are right-handed, and vice versa. Applying each of your hands to a task normally done only with one or the other boosts both hemispheres of the brain, stirring and internalizing surprising layers of buried memory. It can in fact serve as a type of therapy, especially when significant memories have been long obscured or suppressed.

Here's one way of putting this to work:

Call to mind a problem that's been troubling you of late. (Leave aside the major life crises for now. You can work up to those.) Now write it down in the form of a question, using your dominant hand.

Pass the pen to your nondominant hand and write the answer.

Though this may feel awkward at first, as you keep it up, you will probably arrive at astoundingly helpful new thoughts and ideas.

Next try asking yourself questions about unresolved emotions in your life. You may be surprised by the wise person within who shows up with answers.

Another method is to draw a picture of yourself as a child with your nondominant hand and have a conversation with her. Your dominant hand has spent years in school and is well-trained as to how to cross a T or dot an I. But your nondominant hand is like a little child who hasn't been conditioned to perform according to others' expectations. This is a way to gain access to that inner child.

Your nondominant hand is like a little child who hasn't been conditioned to perform according to others' expectations. This is a way to gain access to that inner child.

When I get in touch with my little girl, she's a hopeless romantic, still dancing along diamond-studded sidewalks with her father. She loves nothing more than to watch a Julia Roberts movie and cry her eyes out. In every interaction, she's looking for romance and passion and glamour. She wants to be adored unconditionally, stay young and gorgeous forever, and have it all. She is always searching for perfection, knowing full well that perfection is a hope, a dream, and an illusion. It leaves a heavy place in her heart, a hurt she desperately wants to heal, or at least ignore. But she can't.

Some measure of pain or longing or heaviness is inherent in the human condition. Our lives are imperfect, and too often flat and boring. We can easily drift into negativity, then decide we have made terrible mistakes—wrong house, wrong job, wrong spouse—and become unmotivated, miserable, resentful, or judgmental.

Of course, it's all true. Until we realize that it's not. We can catch ourselves and remember that 75 percent of our thoughts are negative and that the challenge is to rise above the pain, or rather to feel it and move past it toward greater positivity. So we take a deep breath, choose some tool or other that brings us back to pleasant feelings and a positive outlook, and move on. It might last an hour, maybe a day or more, until the heaviness returns. And so it goes, day after day.

A tad hyperbolic, perhaps, but that's the dance of life, and to one degree or another we all know the moves. That may very well be why you are reading this book, seeking to break free from those heavy places. Some do it with drugs or food. Or with movies or romantic encounters or obsessive exercise. Others take refuge in their careers and the drive to get ahead, or through ostensibly selfless devotion to family, community, a religion, or a cause.

But my little girl knows there is no escape. She knows that sometimes we must fake it until we make it. And that sometimes we lose, for days or weeks or months. Then the tools set forth in this book become ever more precious. Nobody is happy all the time. My little girl knows that.

Your inner child is always in your corner to dress the cuts and bruises between rounds, to help you brush off the insults and injuries and send you back fighting into the ring. Every self-coach needs a cheerleader (read: inner child) rooting for her to do the right thing. Which also means thinking the right thing. "Is there such a thing, as the right thing?" you may ask.

Excuses versus Affirmations

Some thoughts make us stronger, happier, calmer, and more solution-oriented. These thoughts bespeak emotional intelligence. They keep us motivated, positive, in flow. They make us more consistently functional and inspire us to get things done. More specifically, they're the thoughts that remind you that you are loveable, and capable, that there are good people in your life who are ready to be allies, not enemies. When you remind yourself that there's no other place quite like this place, and there's no time like the present, you'll know beyond a doubt that you must be in the right place at the right time, and therefore you can pass the test.

Coaches know that positive affirmations can sometimes bring up more resistance than inspiration. But a self-coach schooled in the art of writing down affirmations with a non-dominant hand is a self-coach empowered with an inner child.

Many of us believe that we are all responsible for our actions and our words. Others, equally intelligent, believe that we have little or no control over our thoughts. Both are true. There is what is termed an *initial thought*, the one that comes to mind uninvited. It is a by-product of our life experiences, our families of origin, our report cards from third grade or junior high, the information we've absorbed and the self-images we have formulated from then till now. But once we become aware of this default thinking and its impact on our feelings and our actions, we realize that we can choose our thoughts.

We have little or no control over the initial thought, but we can decide whether we want to dance with it, wine and dine it, and offer it a prominent place in our ruminations. Once you remember that 75 percent of your thoughts are negative and/ or habitual, and that feelings aren't facts, you can choose to replace the initial thought with a more positive one that will produce the desired outcome.

We have little or no control over the initial thought, but we can decide whether we want to dance with it, wine and dine it, and offer it a prominent place in our ruminations.

It's helpful to have a storehouse of positive thoughts etched into your consciousness. Do you remember sitting on the beach at the edge of the shoreline digging little channels in the sand? Did you notice how the water traveled easily into those rivulets, into those prefabricated paths of least resistance? Now try applying the same principle to creating conduits for more positive thinking. Take some time to reinforce your neural pathways toward positivity—playfully. Develop healthy thinking habits, again, by writing down affirmations with your nondominant hand.

Perhaps your initial thought is "I can't do this; it's too hard for me." There are a million excuses built into such an emotional cul-de-sac. Some of the more common ones: it's too risky. It will take a long time. I don't deserve it. I can't afford it. I'm not smart enough or strong enough. I'm too old or too young. I don't have the energy. There will be family drama. I have no one to help me. Or I'm just plain scared! If any of this sounds familiar and has stopped you from achieving something in the past, it's time to overpower those excuses and move on. You can stay stuck and find a hundred reasons not to achieve your goal. (They're on sale, marked down from a million.) Or you can coach yourself, nudge yourself on, by choosing an encouraging, liberating affirmation.

In his classic work on positive motivation, *Excuses Begone*, Wayne Dyer suggests such affirmations as:

I can accomplish anything I choose.
I am a worthy and valuable person.
I am intellectually capable.
I deserve the best because I am good.
I attract abundance in all areas of my life.
I deserve health, happiness, and success.
I am loved by others, and I love myself.
I am independent enough not to rely on the opinions of others.

This last one is particularly critical for me. Having been raised by a loving mom who repeatedly asked me, "How did they think you looked?" I am very vulnerable to the judgments of others. I've learned to work it down with a lot of deep breathing, dancing, and quietly empowering self-talk. But the challenge remains huge.

One more favorite: *I don't have to be better than anyone else, just better than I was yesterday.*

Find a quiet place where you will not be distracted. Meditate for a few minutes, breathing deeply and mindfully. Then write each of these affirmations five times with your nondominant hand. Some may speak to you more than others. That's OK. Let your whole brain get into the act. After all, your negative self-opinions have been etched into your brain for years!

I highly endorse this exercise and encourage you to repeat it as often as needed. When you can overcome an outdated self-image, you can free yourself from constraint and get excited about your life. Let your imagination flow. Enthusiasm always trumps excuses. And remember: the only basket that is never scored is the one that is never shot.

Music Makes the World Go Round

Music produces a kind of pleasure
which human nature cannot do without.
—Confucius

Life seems to go on without effort when I am filled with music.
—George Eliot

For some of us it was the Back Street Boys, or Celine Dion, or Adele. For others it was the Beatles, the Grateful Dead, Bob Dylan. Generations come and go, but the magic is nonstop: music has a remarkable ability to evoke emotions, trigger memories, and create a sense of connection—all of which significantly influence our moods and have a profound impact on happiness and well-being. Upbeat, lively songs lead to feelings of happiness, energy, and positivity, while soothing melodies or music with sentimental value conjure up calm and contentment. Certain songs or genres have the power to resonate deeply with our innermost emotions. Lyrics, melodies, rhythm, and other untold elements mirror our feelings and the thoughts that spawn them.

When I feel a little low or know I have a lot of busywork to accomplish, I turn to Spotify to keep me sane. Good speakers are a great investment. As I fill the house with oldies from my formative years, I find myself transported to those days of unbridled idealism and intoxicating freedom. I dance around the house with nary a care and a wealth of newfound energy.

As I fill the house with oldies from my formative years, I find myself transported to those days of unbridled idealism and intoxicating freedom.

Psychological research has supported the idea that music can cue particularly vivid and emotional memories. Studies have shown that people reengage with favorite music more frequently than with favorite books or movies over their lifetimes. Popular music arouses more detailed and evocative memories than photographs of famous faces. Listening to music elicits more positive socially shared memories than watching TV.

Reexperiencing this music appears to particularly intensify memories of our teenage years. Since adolescence is a critical period for exploring and developing one's personal identity, this may begin to explain the link between music and self-defining memories. If you want to change your present mental state or restore the once vibrant self-image of your younger years, turn on something packed with nostalgia and watch the thoughts and feelings flow.

In some cases, music can enhance productivity and focus. Many people find that listening to music while working or studying helps them concentrate better and maintain a positive mindset. One of my sons was struggling with ADHD and too-long school days. I brought in a colleague with impressive credentials in behavioral therapy to speak with his teachers. Her first suggestion was to allow him to listen to music on his noise-canceling headphones while doing individual work in class. Unfortunately, the school was having none of that, and what a shame it was. Music has been shown to reduce stress levels by lowering cortisol (the stress hormone) and triggering the release of dopamine (the "feel-good" neurotransmitter). Tranquil music calms the mind and promotes relaxation. Imagine an eleven-year-old doing math in a state of mellow exhilaration—how much greater would be his chances of success!

Whether attending concerts, singing together, or discussing favorite songs and performers, sharing musical moments creates social bonds and a sense of belonging, which makes good memories. That weekend back at Woodstock; Taylor Swift's Eras Tour; the epic Rolling Stones appearance in Rio. The unity of the crowd was palpable, remember? And that school production you sang in in high school? Wow, like yesterday.

Moreover, engaging with music, whether as a listener or playing an instrument, has been linked to physical health benefits, such as lower blood pressure, reduced heart rate, and improved immune function. When our bodies feel better, we're happier, and vice versa. While attending my online Happiness Studies coursework. I often played ambient music in the background as a way of enhancing a contemplative mindset. And it's an entirely different sort of experience to sit still, eyes closed, focusing fully on the music and only the music.

Creating or performing music can serve as an outlet for self-expression, helping sensitive souls channel their emotions positively and find fulfillment. I miss those moments in our first years of marriage when my husband would serenade me with his guitar for hours nearly every night. We'll get back there soon.

"Dance is the most powerful exercise for increasing happiness," says Tal Ben-Shahar. "It's very difficult to dance and be somber. We usually can't help but smile when we shake our bodies to the beat of our favorite music."

A well-known, very popular healer from overseas used to visit Miami each winter. One year I was very curious to check out his wise ways, but there wasn't much discretionary income at the time to schedule a session. So I thoroughly interrogated my friends who had. He had offered an appropriate astute solution to each of them, but there was one piece of advice virtually everyone received: he would end each session by telling them to dance in their room every night for fifteen minutes.

That is my suggestion to you as well. Regardless of personal taste, the powerful connection between music and happiness remains a universally beneficial phenomenon. As Henry David Thoreau wrote, "When I hear music, I fear no danger. I am invulnerable. I see no foe. I am related to the earliest times, and to the latest."

Happier Eating

Food! Glorious food! One of life's greatest pleasures—and biggest challenges. Clinical findings show that people with a healthy relationship with food think about eating 10–20 percent of the time. Nearly twenty million cookbooks fly off the shelves in America each year. Note the percentage of food pictures on your Instagram or Facebook or family chat. And how about the ubiquitous question: "What are you making for the holidays?" Whence the fascination? When is it ever enough?

A child is born and comes into the world empty, yearning for comfort. He cries, and his mother takes him to her breast. He experiences the sweet taste of mother's milk as he is cradled into her warm and loving flesh. He suckles until satisfied and sinks into a blissful sleep. Ah, so *this* is life!

We spend the next ninety years trying to reproduce that first feeling of fulfillment. We eat too much, we eat too often, we eat too many sweets. We vow that tomorrow will be a better day. Some of us avoid gluten and artificial additives, others avoid animal products or nightshades, but we all have a food thing going on.

While I don't feel comfortable recommending a particular food regimen (there is no one-size-fits-all formula), I feel compelled to mention the findings of the Blue Zones studies. *National Geographic* financed an analysis of communities around the world with the highest concentration of centenarians. There is a common theme regarding food: moderate caloric intake, and a primarily plant-based diet. Even so, whether you are into the Mediterranean diet, the Zone, Keto, or intermittent fasting, you will be happier if you eat according to your values. Guilt is a difficult spice to digest. So are foods that you're told are good for you but that you dislike. Empower yourself! The choice is yours.

Whether you are into the Mediterranean diet, the Zone, Keto, or intermittent fasting, you will be happier if you eat according to your values. Guilt is a difficult spice to digest.

No pressure, but here are some foods that have been empirically demonstrated to promote a good mood. Select the ones that appeal to you:

- Bananas and turkey produce a brain chemical, tryptophane, that regulates mood.
- Berries create a substance like valproic acid, which is a prescription mood-stabilizing drug.
- Quinoa contains quercetin, which is an antidepressant.
- Dark chocolate is filled with antioxidants and reduces cortisol, the stress hormone.
- Salmon is rich in omega-3 fatty acids, which are known to improve mood and fight depression.
- Turmeric is rich in curcumin, which is an anti-inflammatory and reduces anxiety.
- Apples have a calming effect and produce more energy.
- Spinach is rich in folic acid, which reduces fatigue and depression.
- Mushrooms are high in vitamin D, which is particularly important for vegans.
- Coffee and green tea improve cognition, reduce risk for depression, and improve exercise performance.

- Beans are high in magnesium, calming the mind and nervous system.
- Walnuts are rich in plant-based omega-3 and antioxidants.
- Oranges increase collagen production, which decreases wrinkles. That should make you happy.
- Eggs are high in choline, which boosts memory.

There's another kind of food that makes us happy: comfort food. While most people hear that term and automatically think pasta or pizza, comfort foods can just as easily be pickles or cabbage soup if that's where your free association leads you. Foods signify different things for each of us. Specific foods are linked to specific people, triggering memories unique to the individual. Comfort foods are artifacts from our past, memories of wonderful times. If your childhood birthday parties were joyous occasions, you'll likely crave birthday cake or something similar. If your happy times were at Uncle Avi's barbecues with family and fireworks, hot dogs with sauerkraut or sweet relish will be bring satisfaction to your wounded heart. By eating meals that are reminiscent of our good old days, we symbolically raid a refrigerator well stocked with happiness and homemade dopamine.

But don't get too comfortable. You will be healthier if you eat only until you are 75 percent full. I like to apply the metaphor of a washing machine. You can have a top-of-the-line appliance with the most efficient detergent, and yet if you stuff the machine so full that it can hardly rotate, your clothes won't come out clean. Similarly, if you overeat, regardless of the quality of your food, it will be difficult to digest and challenging to metabolize.

The Wheel of Life

Before I began my serious coach training, I came upon a sixteen-hour course for a minimal fee that would provide me with a somewhat sketchy coaching certification. Looking back, I shudder at the thought that anyone could be certified to help others navigate the deep recesses of their lives and loves with sixteen hours of training. But I figured I had been a school principal, a spiritual advisor, and a community service person for many decades, so how much more could I need to know? I signed up and showed up. And although it was far too superficial for a "professional," the training offered one practice that I offer my clients to this day. My friend Sara, a master chef, says that a cookbook is worthwhile if you find just one recipe that you can use successfully.

The technique is called the Wheel of Life. The original wheel is attributed to the late Paul Meyer, who was a thought leader and coaching pioneer in the 1960s. The technique has since been written up and translated into twenty languages. The Wheel of Life helps individuals assess their degree of satisfaction across multiple aspects of life and visualize the relative balance among them. It gives us insights into our overall sense of well-being and identifies areas that could be improved. Here's a step-by-step guide on how to create and use the Wheel of Life.

1. **Identify key life areas.** Begin by defining the key areas of life that are essential for your well-being. Common areas include career, finances, health, family and relationships, personal growth, fun and recreation, physical environment, and spirituality. Other possible categories might be home environment,

self-care, time management, stress management, and communication skills. You can customize the areas based on your specific needs and goals.

Lately I've been doing the exercise with the five SPIRE elements taught by Tal Ben-Shahar—the spiritual, physical, intellectual, relational, and emotional aspects of life. As a sixth
slice, I add "managerial"—how successfully am I keeping it all
together? Are there specific methods, like habit stacking or
reminders, that I could or should be using?

2. **Create the wheel.** Draw a circle and divide it into six or eight
sections, each representing one of the identified life areas (see
next page). The circle resembles a pie chart, and each section
should be labeled with the corresponding area of life, for example, spiritual, physical, intellectual, relational, emotional, and
managerial. You may want to emphasize a more specific aspect,
such as family time, or community service, or finances, career
building, nutrition, or fitness. What six or eight areas are most
important to you?

As you can see, the wheel is highly adaptable to your individual needs. If you don't feel confident drawing one, there are
oodles of downloadable versions. I have included a blank sample
of the wheel on the next page to make it easier to understand. I
tell my clients to print it out and work with pen or pencil for a
more meaningful experience.

3. **Rate satisfaction.** Rate your current level of satisfaction in
each area on a scale from 1 to 10, with 1 being extremely dissat-
isfied and 10 being completely satisfied. For example, 1 would
be a dot closest to the center of the circle, 10 would be the outer

NAME: _____   **DATE:** _____

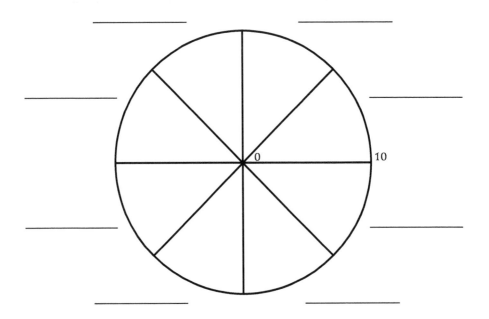

WHEEL OF LIFE INSTRUCTIONS

The 8 sections of the Wheel represent your
present assessment of how satisfied you
are in 8 aspects of your life.

* Please name each section so that it's
  meaningful for you. Ex: **Spirituality,
  Health, Relationships, Work** . . .

* Next, taking the center of the wheel as 0
  and the outer edge as 10, rank your **level
  of satisfaction** in each section on a scale
  of 1 to 10. Draw a straight or curved line
  to create a new outer edge (see example
  at right.)

* This tool will guide us in focusing on
  goals. Together we can make the ride
  less bumpy.

EXAMPLE

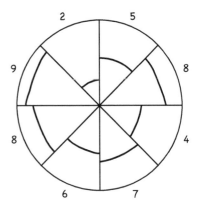

edge. These measurements are about *your* relationship with that area. In other words, if your section is *family*, it's not about how kind or compassionate or successful your family is, but rather, how do you evaluate yourself regarding your personal attention and accomplishments? Do you take the time to connect with your family regularly? Do you make lunch dates with the sister with whom there's a history of some rough edges? Do you call your grandma, or send recipes to your beloved cousin? Have you forgiven your uncle who embarrassed you last Thanksgiving? What can you do to make those relationships healthier? How much effort are you expending? Place a dot or mark along the edge of each section that reflects your current level of satisfaction with your performance.

4. **Draw an arc in each section.** After rating each area, draw an arc based on the number you assigned to that category, creating a jagged or not so jagged line within the circle. This line will represent your own Wheel of Life. The shape of the resulting wheel will indicate the overall balance and satisfaction in your life.

5. **Analyze the results.** Analyze the completed Wheel of Life. Does the picture seem to be in balance overall? If not, which areas are rated unusually high or low on the 1–10 scale? Think into the possible reasons behind your rating and explore your emotional responses to the quantitative assessments. This is a ripe opportunity to gain insight into your active emphases, and to what extent they reflect your core values.

6. **Set goals.** Identify areas that need improvement, or more attention, based on the Wheel of Life assessment. Set specific

and achievable goals for each area. These goals should be challenging but realistic.

7. **Action plan.** Develop a plan of action to address the improvements that you see as called for. Break down the goals into smaller, incremental steps. Try to determine the resources and support required, and to the best of your ability at this point, project a timeline that's both ambitious and realistic (as difficult as that may seem.)

8. **Regular review.** The Wheel of Life is a dynamic tool that can be used over time to track progress and reassess life satisfaction. Revisit the exercise regularly (say monthly or quarterly) to monitor your growth and adjust your goals as necessary.

The Wheel of Life is a particularly effective self-coaching tool. It visually represents the various dimensions of an individual's life, and encourages a balanced, whole-systems approach to goal setting and personal development. When the wheel is more balanced and well-rounded, your travels through life will be less bumpy. Most significantly, the wheel is rooted in one's self-knowledge, and by the same token deepens and enhances self-knowledge in greater and greater detail.

Every time I write or speak about wheels, I always feel compelled to revisit an old familiar parable about a stagecoach. Feel free to steal it and make it your own:

A man is walking by the side of the road. He is carrying a heavy burden. A kindhearted stagecoach driver spots him and offers him a ride, and he gratefully climbs aboard. After a while the driver notices that the man is sitting hunched over with his arms wrapped tightly around his heavy load, and generously invites him to put the bundles down on the seat next to him. The passenger hesitates and declines, saying, "Thank you, but I wouldn't want to burden you." To which the driver replies with a smile, "Sir, my coach is carrying it all for you anyway. Please do let down the load."

There are times when we walk through life carrying a burden so heavy that it saps all our strength and slows us down. That's when we need to give it over to God as we understand Him or to the cosmic flow of the universe. If our burdens are too heavy, we simply cannot function. We need to let them go.

Be Accountable

Speaking of hitching a ride, here's another great initiative to help you realize you dreams. An accountability partner can help you stay on track as you're working toward achieving your goals. An accountability relationship is a mutual partnership in which you and your partner agree to check in regularly and exchange honest feedback.

When I was becoming a coach, I collaborated with a fellow high-school principal named Michael. Every Monday we would set an expectation for the week, such as a reading assignment or making five promotional phone calls. The following Monday we'd report on our progress. Michael had fewer distractions in his life. He wasn't managing a household or newly married, as I was. He was also a more concrete, linear thinker, while I am a random, universal type. I often had to scramble to meet my deadline the night before our meeting, but I got it done. Our partnership kept me on track.

Nonetheless, it was ultimately my responsibility to make sure I reached my goals.

Here are a few tips you might consider to succeed in setting up a program of mutual accountability:

Make a plan. You and your partner should discuss your respective goals, project an ideal timeline, outline the necessary steps, and compare preferred methods of communicating. For example, decide whether you will meet up in person or update each other via email or text. To succeed, you need a system to check in with each other on a regular basis. Having a concrete plan will help you to get moving and avoid procrastination. Brainstorm to create a plan on which you can both agree.

Be open and flexible. Finding an accountability partner with the same goal or similar interests can be useful, but it's not necessary. The right person may or may not have achieved the same level of success or progress as you have until now. Either way is OK. They might have strengths and weaknesses that differ from your own. If each of you brings a unique perspective to the relationship, this could help you see your challenges in a new light and increase your chances for success.

Be realistic. Your accountability partner should be positive and supportive, and yet simultaneously have the courage to call you out when you are slacking. It's preferable to choose someone outside your family, since a family member might not hold you to your goals (or other possible complications), although I might mention that two of my grandsons, first cousins and childhood friends, have been successfully working together for years.

I've long thought that the primary reason for the success of the Weight Watchers program is accountability. It's much harder to finish that carton of ice cream or binge on homemade brownies still warm from the oven with the knowledge that in five days you'll be hopping on a scale in the presence of all your calorie counting colleagues.

The Vision Board

The only thing worse than being blind
is having sight but no vision.
—HELEN KELLER

The mind's eye is a powerful tool. Seeing your dreams and aspirations before you, even if only in the imagination, can help clarify your goals, bring into focus what you want to achieve, and reinforce your commitment. Even those who are most adept at conjuring up a compelling vision out of thin air will benefit with a vision board. When it comes to creating what we want to create in the "real world," manifesting our innermost heart's desire, there's nothing quite as helpful as seeing actual physical representations of our dreams that are visible to the eye.

Constructing a vision board is a creative and tangible way to manifest your goals and desires, and it's so much fun. All that cutting and pasting brings me right back to first grade. I put on a musical "happy mix" from Spotify and if it's late enough in the day, I might complement my project with a lovely glass of dry red wine. My vision boards have stimulated the renovation of my backyard and swimming pool, a stronger commitment to exercising at home, two published books, and a trip to Guatemala. One board hangs above my workspace. It features motivational symbols like a trip to Colorado, the beautiful horse I'll buy when my book becomes a best seller, and a picture of Oprah, who will be promoting my book to her audience(s). I am looking at it now. Another pair of visuals are attached to my fridge with magnets. They beckon me to Costa Rica and again to Guatemala—perhaps to create retreats there, or perhaps just to chill.

My vision boards have stimulated the renovation of my backyard and swimming pool, a stronger commitment to exercising at home, two published books, and a trip to Guatemala.

Steps to Creating a Vision Board

1. **Gather supplies.** Acquire a board (corkboard, a thin piece of plywood, or poster board, which is most accessible and easiest to work with); scissors, glue, and/or tape; magazines, printed images, markers, stickers, or whatever decorative items stir your spirit.

2. **Reflect and set intentions.** Think about your goals, dreams, and aspirations in different areas of your life, such as career, relationships, health, and travel. Consider what you intend to achieve in both the short term and long term.

3. **Collect visuals.** Look through magazines, print out images from the Internet, or select photos from your own collection

that represent your goals. These can include words, phrases, images, or symbols that resonate with you and reflect your aspirations.

4. **Arrange and create.** Cut out the images and arrange them on your board. You can organize them by theme, timeline, or however feels most meaningful to you. Get creative with the layout—add colors, drawings, or inspirational quotes to personalize it further. I like to bathe mine in a wash of watercolors. The one that stimulated my renovated backyard fairyland is sprinkled with pink glitter. But that's just me—you may prefer something more organic.

5. **Display and review.** Place your vision board in a visible spot where you'll see it frequently—your bedroom, office, your fridge, or any place you spend a lot of time. Take a few moments regularly to look at it, visualize your goals, and reaffirm your intentions.

How Vision Boards Help

Here are some of the major benefits of a vision board:

Clarity and focus. Creating a vision board helps clarify your goals and brings focus to what you want to achieve. When you see your aspirations visually represented, it fortifies your intention.

Visualization and manifestation. Visualization is a key to success in any creative endeavor. By regularly visualizing your goals with the aid of your vision board, you reinforce the power of your desires, which can help manifest them into reality. When my husband and I were writing our first book, I designed a book cover and placed it on the outside of the loose-leaf notebook that housed our writing. When I picked it up, I imagined our book displayed in all the airports, next to best sellers like *Atomic Habits*, *Blink*, and *Option B*.

Motivation and inspiration. Visualization serves as a constant reminder and motivator. It can encourage you to take steps towards your goals and define them in greater and greater detail, even on challenging days.

Positive mindset. Engaging with your vision board can foster a positive mindset. It encourages optimism and a belief (make that certainty!) that your goals are achievable.

While a vision board can be a helpful tool, it's important also to take action and work toward your goals assiduously. The board serves as a visual guide and motivator, but you still need to put in the effort and take steps with unflagging determination to achieve what you desire.

Everybody's Got an Angel

There always seems to be someone who shows up in our lives at just the right time, with just the right suggestion. For me one of those people is Bev. I first met her when we were running the Chabad House in Pittsburgh. She had just completed a one-year meditation course at Maharishi International University in Iowa. A well-meaning mutual friend who was aware of our meditation connection thought a taste of Shabbos might be good for her. We clicked immediately, and Bev became a part of our family, and the organizer of the unorganized at our Chabad office. Being an unquenchable spiritual seeker, she was observing the Sabbath and studying Jewish mysticism before long.

One day she disappeared. That wasn't her style, and I was concerned. I walked around the corner to the bank where her sister Karen worked to ask about her. Karen told me she had gone west to take a course somewhere. That didn't jibe, because Bev would certainly have told us her plans. I pressed a bit harder, and Karen reluctantly told me that Bev's parents had swept her off to a deprogrammer in the Midwest. Deprogrammers were a phenomenon that desperate parents employed, during the time that cults were popular, to psychologically manipulate their kids back to what mom and dad thought was "normal." Bev's deprogramming remains one of the top ten traumas of my life. How could her parents think Judaism was a cult? And how could they justify squelching their child's values? I was assured it was done with love, but sadly, from that point forward Bev no longer lived at our house or hung around at the office.

Our friendship remained intact, albeit diluted by time and space. Bev married and had a child and moved to Maryland. We would exchange greetings for the holidays and an occasional recipe, or an "I can't handle life anymore" phone call. One day she called to say she was interested in becoming an administrator in a private Jewish day school in Florida. It seemed like a beautiful place to live, and she wanted her daughter to have a Jewish identity. I made a phone call or two and directed her to the HR person at the school where I was teaching. She was fabulously qualified, and in no time was hired as my principal! Bev was innovative, brilliant, and dedicated. She made wonderful changes to the educational system, and I benefited by receiving amazing training opportunities at Harvard, at the PassageWorks Institute in Boulder, and other cutting-edge programs. She believed in me, and a few years later when she was ready to move on to a yet more prestigious school, she handed over the leadership position to me. It would never have happened otherwise. These schools rarely promote someone from the teaching ranks to administrative positions. They prefer to import an unknown with a PhD from somewhere far away to take the helm.

A couple of years passed, and Bev called again to say she had grown weary of the 7 a.m. to 10 p.m. life of a principal, and she was pursuing a new career as a life coach. She explained to me how life-changing coaching could be, and how she felt this was an opportunity to make a real difference in peoples' lives. No more showing up at the office. This was about showing up in someone's struggles, throwing him a lifeline, and leading him to shore in a way that really speaks to him as an individual.

Bev offered me a few complimentary coaching sessions, and the rest is history. I started training as a coach, and two years later finished my certification in an internationally certified coaching program Bev had founded, tailored to the coaching of the families of addicts. She believes that the family is the addict's best chance of recovery. Her effective program, Family Recovery Resources, has trained hundreds of coaches and helped thousands of families.

Not only did I have the best teachers and mentors in my training, but I was placed in a small learning group with a recovered beer-guzzling air conditioner salesman from the Midwest, a priest with a sex addiction, and a former centerfold Playboy Bunny. My understanding of humanity expanded exponentially as I interacted with my strange bedfellows and cultivated a true appreciation and respect for individuals from wildly divergent backgrounds. And I learned so much about myself! This was the germinal stage in what became my passion and purpose—teaching people how to coach themselves.

PART TWO

People Who Love People

9

Lovers, Friends, and Family

Most of my clients come bringing this, that, or the other specific issue, be it anxiety, or a negative self-image, or a subconscious tendency to self-sabotage. But virtually *all* my clients are looking for deeper, more lasting, more seamless relationships with the people who really matter in their lives.

As they most definitely should.

The longest-ever longitudinal study of human emotions is the Harvard Study of Adult Development, begun in 1938, during the Great Depression. Some 268 Harvard sophomores volunteered to be subjects of the study. Over the next seventy-five years, the researchers followed the subjects' lives, hoping to discover clues to the factors that lead to living healthy and happy lives. Among the recruits were such notables as the future U.S. president John F. Kennedy and the journalist who eventually became the storied editor of *The Washington Post*, Ben Bradlee.

Over time the study expanded to include some 1300 offspring of the original participants, many now in their fifties and sixties, to track the extent to which early-life experiences affect health and aging over time. Some grew to become successful businessmen, doctors, and lawyers, while others struggled to make a living and raise a family, often grappling with mental health issues and addiction. Through the years the control groups expanded to include 456 inner-city residents of Boston, and later their wives as well. Researchers studied their health patterns and their overall life experiences in detail, including the various successes and failures in their personal and professional lives.

The study revealed that far more than money or fame or extraordinary talent, overwhelmingly it is *close relationships* that keep people happy throughout their lives. Those loving ties protected the Harvard men, as well as the inner-city participants, and proved a far stronger predictor of health, happiness, and longevity than social class, bank balances, IQ, or even genes.

Having good relationships is not only good for our bodies, but also for our brains. Noteworthy, too, was the discovery that having *higher-quality* close connections is more important than the *number* of friends one has. One or two solid buddies, or a dedicated spouse, can be enough. "The good life," Robert Waldinger, director of the Harvard study, wrote, "is built with good relationships." Moreover, "a troubled marriage can be as hazardous to physical health as cigarette smoking."

I tell my clients that they can change their relationships with or without any help from their partners, children, or colleagues at work. It may take two to tango, but it only takes one to spread the love, increase the peace, and make it better. I have a cardboard sign attached to the white wicker mirror in my bedroom that says, "I create love in the world." There are, of course, relationships that are so tainted with dysfunction that even Harry Houdini couldn't make the magic last. But for most of us, a few proactive adjustments can do wonders.

It may take two to tango, but it only takes one to spread the love, increase the peace, and make it better.

An essential objective of the work we put forth in these pages is the cultivation of self-love. Not in the sense of narcissism—I don't expect that you'll be gazing at your image in the lake and swooning—rather, that you will be able to see your reflection in the mirrors of all your relationships with greater self-esteem. And no, not because you're fit and trim, or because your teeth are whiter or your skin more radiant, but because you are coming ever closer to your essential you. As such, you have less need to impress and more ability to express. Because you love yourself more, you can love your nearest and dearest more as well. They in turn will feel that love and reciprocate.

There is a biblical adage that encourages us to "Love your neighbor as yourself." Not so grand or challenging a goal, is it? But what if you *don't* love yourself?

10

To Know and Be Known

We fool ourselves into thinking we are hungry for validation. Truth be told, we are hungry to know and be known. We want authentic relationships wherein we love and are loved for who we really are. That takes work and awareness. No ego games or needier-than-thou competition. Your focus is on whether you're being a grown-up or not. Children need validation. They like things to be easy and to go the way they want. They like to know that there are adults around to soothe them and kiss their booboos. What if you could learn to like yourself, to feel good about yourself, without requiring someone else's praise and compliments?

Such growth takes hard work, and the reward is a kind of intimacy that helps you be more of the person you want to be. It supports the development of deep lifelong bonds. You are seen, known, and understood for who you truly are. Not to mention loved and desired. In this vein, here's another book recommendation for self-coachers who aim high: David Schnarch's *Pas-*

sionate Marriage: Keeping Love and Intimacy Alive in Committed Relationships.

Social intercourse calls for vulnerability. It's about getting over yourself and merging passionately, openly, with the people you are meant to love. That includes your mate, your mother, your child, your business partner, your neighbor, and your best friend. It means letting go of fear and judgment, realizing that there is always enough, so there is no place for envy or rivalry, nor measuring up to anyone else's standards or stature. It means being loving and accepting as well as understanding that other people's lives or the way they hold their fork are none of your business. When you understand that the only person you can change is yourself, you begin to see others in a different light. No one hired you to be the feature film critic for *The New Yorker* (although my first cousin David Denby was for nearly twenty years). No one asks you how many thumbs up your kid deserves: he deserves your full attention and support. Not the gnawing "How are others going to see him?" Not the well-meaning, "How's about I drive you to the gym?" or "Maybe you should eat your salad first?"

When you understand that the only person you can change is yourself, you begin to see others in a different light.

How is it that so many of us become emotionally rigid (if not frigid)? Hiding behind our cell phones, maybe, or lusting after the latest status symbol? Or squandering our talents on the performance of tasks that really don't mean all that much, yet clamor for attention? Why are we so often in a rush to be distracted, obsessively busy, running races that won't reward us even when we win? What happened to just being ourselves, taking our time, happily hanging with friends and family who are only busy being *themselves*?

We don't want excuses. We want relationships.

Many of us make the mistake of thinking that what's important is *finding love*. What's more to the point is *keeping love alive*. Maintaining a relationship. You might find the perfect job, but if you walk in on day one, put your feet up on the desk, and veg out, chances are you won't be on that job for long.

Relationships work the same way. You want a loving relationship? You've got to work for it. Make your relationship a priority. Workaholism, urgent but unimportant tasks, devices with screens, and other distractions can get in the way. Knowing, as we do now, that the most significant barometers of happiness are our genuine connections with others, we need to starve those less significant time gobblers and feed our relationships.

Recently while on a cruise. I met a lovely grandma who was traveling with one of her six grandchildren. She told me she is devoted to spending wonderful alone time with each of them, so she schedules something special with one of them every couple of months. I was so inspired. I hope you are too. Imagine creating that special bonding time with the loved ones in your life (and they need not be relatives.) Commit to quality time together, daily, weekly, monthly. Take on projects together. Have a calling or a fascination that you share. Do fun things and think new thoughts. Fan the spark. Travel together, listen to music together, learn new things together, relax together, and you are not likely to grow apart.

Yes, you say, but it's hard.

Maybe you're expecting too much. Or maybe you're investing too much too dutifully—because if it's not genuine, it's not intimate. Putting on a performance or wearing a mask sucks up a lot of energy and doesn't get you any closer to a real relationship. Can you disclose your fears, your dreams, your secrets? Can you be vulnerable? Can you take responsibility for your own emotions and be comfortable with the fact that your partner, sibling, grandchild, child, or best friend is not your spiritual twin? That means no longer expecting them to automatically validate you or reassure you that you're all right. Is there room in your relationship for a loved one to tell you that sometimes your ideas are not only outside the box but off the wall?

Creating a strong relationship begins with what we *don't* do and *don't* say—in accordance with the time-honored teaching to refrain from saying to another what we wouldn't want said to us. It takes refinement and impulse control to abstain from making judgmental or sarcastic comments, for reminding our spouses of what they didn't get done. It means being cognizant of our tone of voice and our facial expressions, filtering out those almost imperceptible cynical nuances. Even if we never in a million years would have meant it that way, sometimes highly sensitive people will react to insults that aren't really there. Tread lightly and pay attention.

When you know there's a lot of emotion bound up with your message, practice it in front of a mirror a few times first. Something's bothering you? Take a few deep breaths and relax your face and jaw before delivering the goods. When you anticipate some friction, it's also helpful to add a touch of curiosity. Ask questions in a calm tone that says you're looking for a solution rather than a victory.

Allow me to add at this point that there are limits to authenticity. An insincere mask of empathy and respect can be far better than a sincere gesture of intolerance and disgust. Our emotions are fickle, our thoughts even more so. Sometimes we're just in an ugly mood. It's been said that 75 percent of our thoughts are negative, and that life is more beautiful when we don't act on them. Impulse control is essential.

Going a step beyond the Golden Rule—*do not do to another what you wouldn't want done to you*—Tal Ben-Shahar posits the Titanium Rule: *do not do or say to those close to you what you would never say or do to the stranger who is far away*. Before delivering your daily 5 p.m. faultfinding report, stop and consider whether you would be so bold as to make the same disparaging comments to an associate at the office: "Why must you look so unkempt? Can you grab a snack without ransacking the kitchen? When was the last time you went to the gym?"

Positive, purposeful interactions are the vitamins that keep relationships healthy. Just as vitamins are most effective when taken regularly, it would be wise to make these interactions into rituals: very precise behaviors, performed at very specific times, motivated by deeply held values, to help a relationship flourish.

As I mentioned earlier, establishing a new ritual can be complicated, but maintaining it becomes comparatively easy when the intention is clear. Wednesday night date night, board games on Saturday afternoon, or an early beach walk every Sunday are game changers. How about doing a little sunrise yoga with your spouse while the house is still asleep?

You might also get into the habit of calling or texting friends and family with loving messages. Technology really does its job when it is used to unify us rather than distract us. Our family has a WhatsApp group that shares good news in South Africa, Israel, New York, Florida, and California simultaneously and daily. One of the group rules is that the negative stuff doesn't go onto the group chats. A little negative barb online can sting all the way until the next opportunity to work it down in person. There's been a lot of focus on cyberbullying and its effects; I'm not sure how much energy has gone into researching the effect of kind and encouraging words online. But I know that when one of my kids says something that makes me feel good, I often scroll back and read it again and again. Ask yourself:

What sort of rituals would you like to introduce between you and a close friend, a child, or a sibling?

Are there meaningful activities you've neglected to engage in together that would improve your bond?

Rather than just thinking about these questions, take a few minutes to write your answers down. That's what coaching yourself is about: I won't be nearby to remind you.

11

Loving-Kindness Meditation

There's a new, updated take on love in the air these days, and it shows up not a moment too soon. Defined in depth by noted research psychologist Barbara Frederickson in her book *Love 2.0: Creating Happiness and Health in Moments of Connection*, it's just the ticket for this often love-challenged day and age.

Frederickson describes this unique characterization of love as, in essence, a momentary flash, a mini moment of what she calls *positivity resonance*. It can happen when you share a smile, a mutually enjoyed experience, or a warm handshake. She likens it to the lyric in Louis Armstrong's classic song, "What a Wonderful World": "I see friends shaking hands, saying, 'How do you do?' They're really saying, 'I love you.'"

"I see friends shaking hands, saying, 'How do you do?' They're really saying, 'I love you.'"

You can share such a moment with a spouse, a sibling, a child, a colleague, or a perfect stranger. It gladdens the heart, sharpens your mind, and activates your vagus nerve. (The vagus nerve, also known as the vagal nerves, regulate your parasympathetic nervous system, which controls body functions such as digestion, heart rate, and immune system.) These minidoses of love produce oxytocin, often referred to as one of the four happy hormones, which give us an overall feeling of calm and stimulate further feelings of kindness and creativity. (The other three are dopamine, serotonin, and endorphins.)

When it comes to cultivating an embodied sense of well-being, love is undeniably the supreme emotion. There are innumerable opportunities every day to experience this type of love, but it's up to you to show up and be both receptive and proactive.

Love 2.0 offers a wonderful technique for honing your love receptors. It's known as the Loving-Kindness Meditation, and you can do it daily:

Find a peaceful corner where you can meditate without interruption. Sit comfortably, with the lower part of your back well supported, and straighten your spine. Lean forward just a bit and pull your shoulders back. This position allows you to expand your rib cage in all directions, creating space around your heart. Place your feet on the floor and your palms on your thighs. Allow your eyes to close.

Breathe into your heart. Notice how each breath brings renewed energy as your heart sends fresh oxygen throughout your body. (Technically it's oxygenated blood, but keep it simple and heartfelt.) Keep this up for several breaths, noticing the sensations in your heart as well as in all your limbs and organs. Now think of someone you love and care for—someone whose face you can visualize and whose endearing qualities come to mind. This will arouse some tender feelings. Stay with that genuine warmth and kindness, and slowly say the following:

May this one (insert name) feel safe.

May this one (insert name) feel happy.

May this one (insert name) be healthy.

May this one (insert name) live with ease.

Imagine what the fulfillment of each of these wishes would look like, feeling the sensations that arise within you. Go slowly and repeat it again. Next, spread these friendly feelings to your family, repeating the loving-kindness wishes for them.

May my family feel safe.

May my family feel happy.

May my family be healthy.

May my family live with ease.

Continue, this time spreading these feelings to your community, to your country, and finally to the entire world. As you end your meditation, remember that you can create these positive feelings whenever you wish. By practicing this meditation, you've begun to condition your emotions to do exactly that. Consequently, you will be more open to the experience of true connection with others.

Stan came to me initially as a client for educational coaching. He is the principal of a midsized private high school. He was interested in exploring effective ways to get his teachers to interact and share their successes and difficulties. Stan is a really bright guy, single, in his late thirties, and good at his job. During our discussion, he told me that he feels isolated at school, even though the faculty, parents, and students like him. He was wrestling with mild depression, and his motivation was low. He felt that his environment was somehow threatening, that he always had to be on his best behavior because everyone was watching. He accomplished everything that was expected from him, and then some, but was experiencing very little enjoyment from it all.

I told him that feeling lonely in a crowd is as bad for his health as smoking cigarettes. I added that it is hard for anyone to be open while always on the lookout for a potential threat. I asked him if he was conscious of making eye contact, deep breathing, and positive self-talk. He laughed so wryly I didn't have to wait for his answer. I offered a suggestion: perhaps he would like to do the Loving-Kindness Meditation from time to time, maybe even regularly, just to open up his love receptors a bit.

After a month or so of meditating a few times a week, he reported that he felt safer at school and was seeking opportunities to interact with his colleagues and the parents. He was beginning to enjoy the witty exchange at the water cooler and the high-fives from the high school kids. Then, every night when he came home, he began calling to mind and writing down two or three pleasant social encounters he had experienced during the day. He was on a roll and feeling good about it.

We didn't continue the coaching relationship for very long after that, but I was convinced that Stan would continue to feel more and more creative in his job and establish deeper relationships with his staff. Sometimes a small adjustment can snowball into a very big difference.

12

Marriage: Oneness and Twoness

To be fully seen by somebody and be loved anyhow—this is a
human offering that can border on miraculous.
—ELIZABETH GILBERT

As a marriage coach, I challenge my clients to believe and appreciate that there is nothing in the world more important than establishing and maintaining an intimate, emotionally healthy marital relationship. Ideally it begins with each partner acknowledging that he/she is the other half of your soul. Commitment follows logically and seamlessly from this mutual understanding.

Ideally it begins with each partner acknowledging that he/she is the other half of your soul.

The second step is to take full responsibility for the things *you* can change in your own attitude and behavior without demanding or expecting change from another.

A good coach holds us accountable for showing up and doing everything we can. When coaching ourselves, we need to first summon that accountability from within ourselves. Self-coaching demands exactly that. And as my husband often reminds me, your spouse is *not* your coach.

As we have seen, the research and data of the Harvard Study of Adult Development, collected over the course of nearly a century, have shown how creating and sustaining a good marriage can be the single most important undertaking in a person's life. The wisdom of traditional cultures that have prevailed over the span of human history tells us the same thing. Of all meaningful relationships (and there are many permutations), marriage is certainly the most fruitful. It is chock-full of opportunities for a couple to help each other reclaim wholeness, heal their inner children (for who among us can claim to be free of childhood wounds?), and experience and express unconditional trust and love. It is our rectification, our prescription for transformation and emotional health. And at the risk of repeating something we've all no doubt heard before (were we listening?), success in marriage, like success in every other important venture, is a function of 5 percent inspiration and 95 percent perspiration.

John Gottman is touted by many as today's foremost expert on relationships. His book *The Seven Principles for Making Marriage Work* has sold over a million copies. Based on his work in his "Love Lab" with more than 650 couples over fifteen years, he was able to predict the marriages that would end in divorce with 91 percent accuracy. Gottman posits that a good or bad marriage is not determined by the number of conflicts a couple deals with. Some of the best marriages have lots of conflict; but they also can make successful repairs. They know how to lighten up when things get heavy. For some, it's a hug. For others, it's sticking out their tongues or asking their mate's opinion about something ridiculously off the topic, just to reengage.

Gottman observed that good marriages are built on (it's a big list):

- Friendship and mutual respect
- Accepting what you cannot change
- Making room for compromise
- Acquiescing to your partner's influence
- Making time for and being patient with each other
- Embracing your partner as an imperfect being
- Creating a shared meaning in a culture rich with symbols and rituals

Good marriages are also based on an appreciation for the roles and goals that link you together. These criteria are applicable to other relationships as well—with children, grown children, close friends, and colleagues at work . . . (Whew! You may want to reread the above list a few times before moving on.)

Gottman maintains that there are two types of marital conflicts—those that can be resolved, and those that are perpetual, which means they will be part of your lives in some form forever. He goes on to say that 69 percent of all conflicts fall into this latter category. In other words, you'll never convince your partner that you're right. And yet many such couples are very happy in their marriages, because they don't allow themselves to be overwhelmed by their differences. They keep their conflicts in perspective and approach them with a sense of humor. Yet still they disagree.

Incidentally, my favorite app on the phone (aside from Uber Eats) is the Gottman Card Decks. It's filled with readily doable suggestions for expressing empathy, communicating needs, conveying appreciation, establishing rituals of connection, and building friendship. Gottman refers to these as "love maps." It's a great app for dating as well.

Together and Apart

The tools for forging a good marriage lie in three distinct spheres: our thoughts, our speech, and our deeds. We can replace divisive or critical thoughts by paying attention to the things we appreciate; we can speak more respectfully and listen more empathically; and we can go out of our way to perform acts of kindness without keeping score or expecting anything in return.

The return on these investments—the fulfillment we will experience—will know no bounds. Marriage is the only relationship in which we can achieve and experience oneness in every dimension of our lives—spiritual, intellectual, emotional, and physical. With practice and commitment, we can cultivate a bond that says loud and clear: *there is no place where "I" end and "you" begin.* What we need to do—what we are uniquely capable of doing—is to bring our vitality, our spirit, and our potency to the space between us, to close off all the emotional energy leaks and become partners for real.

The Nobel Prize-winning Chilean poet Pablo Neruda said it beautifully:

> *I love you without knowing how, or when, or from where,*
> *I love you simply, without problems or pride:*

I love you in this way because I do not know any other
    way of loving but this,
in which there is no I or you;
so intimate that your hand upon my chest is my hand,
so intimate then when I fall asleep your eyes close.

What a magnificent sonnet! Is it achievable? I think so. It calls for committing to uninterrupted quality time together every day, no matter what. Love is something we should recultivate every morning, afternoon, and evening. Many clients lament to me that they have very little in common with the person they married. But if you stop and think about it, it's perfectly insane to expect that men and women will marry and have anything in common at all. Dave Meurer, author of *Good Spousekeeping*, observes: "A great marriage is not when the 'perfect couple' comes together. It is when an imperfect couple learns to enjoy their differences."

The strength of most relationships is not a matter of how like-minded two people are (I don't think very many such twosomes exist) but rather how open they are to each other's differences. From my own experience: a simple word like *dinnertime* can have vastly different connotations. Consider the only child (me) of a conservative Republican stockbroker, with meals elegantly served by the full-time help in our affluent seashore community. Contrast that with the son (my husband) of an anarchist revolutionary poet whose parents were divorced and whose mom was rarely home for dinner. I would come to the table properly dressed and sit for an hour with my parents, conversing about school and politics and community events. My husband would come home to an empty apartment in an urban co-op to find a $5 bill on the table and a note saying, "Get some pizza."

That's just dinnertime. There can be hundreds more similarly incongruent cues throughout the day that would need a whole lot of decoding to explain how any two people constitute a couple.

There's also the fact that I'm an extrovert and my husband is an introvert. That I love dairy, and he prefers meat. That I would love nothing better than a Gypsy Vanner horse, a parti-colored poodle, and a relationship with every stray kitten in the neighborhood, while he thinks other people's pets are more than enough. I'm a hopeless Pollyanna; he has to work on himself to overcome an inbred cynical nature. (To his great credit, he usually succeeds.) I spend money like it's water; he is admirably frugal. I'm a bit over the top and sometimes wildly enthusiastic; he is delightfully reserved and refined. Upon meeting me for the first time, one of my husband's friends said to him, "You didn't tell me you were marrying the Energizer Bunny."

There is a slightly altered version of the famous Serenity Prayer posted on our refrigerator: "God grant me the serenity to accept the *people* I cannot change, the courage to change the *people* I can, and the wisdom to know that those 'people' are *only me*."

"God grant me the serenity to accept the *people* I cannot change, the courage to change the *people* I can, and the wisdom to know that those 'people' are *only me*."

The only person you can change is you. On a deeper level, the only person you should *want* to change is you. Acceptance is a sign of emotional intelligence, and the choice is yours. When we define our happiness in terms of how closely our spouse, best friend, or business partner echoes our sentiments, we are thinking like a victim, abandoning control, assigning our potential for joy to someone else. My daughter dislikes my political persuasion and my views on birth control. But we share a great deal, including the right to respectfully disagree.

"I'm unhappy because of him"? Nuh-uh. We are always at choice, neither stuck nor helpless. I am very happily married to someone who is very far from being my cosmic twin. We are insanely in love, and it keeps getting better. Go figure.

The great German philosopher Arthur Schopenhauer coined a beautiful metaphor for how we navigate our relationships. He called it the "hedgehog's dilemma" (sometimes called the "porcupine dilemma"). In the winter, hedgehogs (or porcupines) need to warm each other to protect themselves from freezing. If they get too close, they will injure each other with their sharp quills. If they remain too distant, on the other hand, they will freeze. Their survival depends on the delicate balance of closeness and distance.

Ours does too. Can we love and merge? Can we love and let go? I've never been comfortable with the concept of codependence, wondering if it cancels out deep empathy and the need to help my mate. If my husband is in a foul mood, can I be elated about life? Am I compassionate or codependent or frozen?

Schopenhauer's model, particularly in marriage, refers to the challenge of balancing intimacy with independence. We're often like those porcupines, seeking warmth in the winter. We might hurt each other if we get too close. In a marriage, or for that matter in any close relationship, individuals crave emotional connection while also valuing their personal space. Too much closeness might lead to conflict or feeling overwhelmed, while too much distance might result in feelings of loneliness or detachment. Striking the right balance between mutual support and autonomy requires understanding, compromise, and respect for each other's boundaries. Knowing that each relationship is unique, keep an eye on how the dynamic fluidity of oneness and twoness plays out in yours.

In a similar vein, here's another take on oneness and twoness from Kahlil Gibran:

> Let there be spaces in your togetherness. And let the winds of the heavens dance between you. Love one another but make not a bond of love: Let it rather be a moving sea between the shores of your souls. Fill each other's cup but drink not from one cup. Give one another of your bread but eat not from the same loaf. Sing and dance together and be joyous, but let each one of you be alone, even as the strings of a lute are alone, though they quiver with the same music. Give your hearts, but not into each other's keeping. For only the hand of Life can contain your hearts. And stand together, yet not too near together: For the pillars of the temple stand apart, and the oak tree and the cypress grow not in each other's shadow.

Rituals of Love

Take a moment to think of the sort of rituals that might help make you and your spouse happier, more mutually accepting. Once you come up with a ritual or two you'd like to implement, write them down in a planner. In fact, write one down *now*, so it won't get misplaced somewhere along the path of good intentions.

Each small, incremental step will unleash a cascade of positive feelings and strengthen your resolve to keep growing in other areas as well. Yes, habits are difficult to change but that very resistance to change becomes advantageous when we are dealing with *good* habits. Remember Aristotle: "Excellence is not an act, but a habit."

A suggestion: Get off the phone when he walks in the door. Your soul mate needs continual reassurance that he is the most important person in your life. I even go so far as to advise clients to *pretend* they're on the phone and then announce with a fanfare "My wife just arrived—I really want to spend time with her!" Although I say it in jest, this is a perfect opportunity to assure your partner that they are the most significant human being in your world. They really are, you know.

While you're busy making things better, it would be wise to admit that *doubt* remains an insidious saboteur. Self-doubt especially can undermine our best efforts to be all that we can be, to achieve our most deeply held hopes and goals. Sometimes, despite all our affirmations and exercises in building self-confidence—*I think I can, I think I can!*—there's a sneaky little voice whispering in the inner ear saying, *Really? Who do I think I'm fooling? I know I can't!* Even when the doubts appear to be focused on others in our lives—*can I trust this person? Is his love true? Is this relationship built on loyalty and love and mutual esteem, or . . . ?*—it's *self-doubt* that lurks beneath these conscious thoughts and keeps us insecure.

Coach yourself by all means. And keep it real. Which means be realistic. All the journaling, affirmations, physical exercise, and self-care can bring us to the level of better, but not perfect. We remain human and flawed. We need to be willing to entertain our unpleasant emotions and doubts, and to understand that they are an inevitable part of the big picture. Then we turn to our mate and say, "I'm only 60 percent today; can you show up with the other 40 percent and help me up?"

For each of us, assurance comes in a different form. Gary Chapman's *Five Languages of Love: The Secret to Love That Lasts* is an amazing read. Chapman postulates that each person has a primary love language that you must learn to speak if you want them to feel loved. Here is a quick synopsis:

- For some, the primary language of love is words of praise and appreciation, **positive verbal reinforcement** that feeds both self and mutual esteem.
- The second love language is **acts of service**. This is the language of those who can be heard saying, "Actions speak louder than words."
- The third language is **gifts**. They need not be expensive. A small bouquet of flowers serves as proof that you're thinking of her when you are not together. (Make them cut flowers rather than perennials. The frequency keeps it fresh.)
- If your partner's love language is **quality time**, your undivided attention is the best way you can show your love. Some guys think they can watch a football game, check out an interesting post on Instagram, and listen to their wives all at the same time. That may well be, but it is not speaking the love language of quality time. Turn

off the TV, put down the smart/stupidphone, and gaze into your mate's eyes. Listen and interact. "Undivided" is the magic word in this equation.

- The last of these languages is **physical touch**. Hugging, kissing, massaging, and sexual intimacy. If this is your spouse's language, the most meaningful expression comes when you initiate the affection.

Whatever the default love language may be, it's important to make eye contact when your spouse is speaking. Stop whatever you are doing, listen, and resist the impulse to interrupt. Seek first to understand, and then to be understood. Learn to become an empathetic listener. Show her that you heard what she was saying by repeating it in your own words and then asking, "Have I got you completely?" or "Have I understood you correctly?" Don't talk to your spouse from another room. Don't allow anything extraneous to vie for your attention.

This was a tough exercise for me, as I am an incessant doer, a multitasker, and rarely a sit-downer. My husband is more given to taking time to investigate the context and gain perspective on situations. He needs to talk things out. At first, sitting in one place and giving him my undivided attention for what seemed like hours was akin to torture. After a while, I realized how much deeper and richer our communication was when we gave it enough time to ripen. As we aired our feelings, pearls of insight and love came to the surface. We gained a level of intimacy I had never imagined possible.

A woman once walked into a department store looking for a new perfume. She told the saleswoman that she wanted something *irresistible*. The saleslady asked, "What should it smell like—blossoms in the spring, a bed of roses, succulent tropical fruits?" "No," she replied. *"Absolutely* irresistible. Like my husband's laptop."

Clocks click swiftly. Calendars even more so. We must work hard to create quality time. Daily, weekly, monthly, on vacation or during staycations, go out together for breakfast or lunch. And leave the screens home. Mornings are often preferable to evening excursions, because you're less likely to be tired or grumpy. Take a walk in nature once a month. Collaborate to make a list of things you'd like to do together, then do them. There is a group on the Internet that challenges married couples to commit to one date per week for the first month and then one per month for the rest of the year. It sounds like a great idea.

Remember to keep your quality time plans realistic and affordable in terms of time and money. It is far better to make small incremental changes that you can sustain than sweeping plans that can't be fulfilled. (Atomic habits.) Quality time is not about being in the same room and distracted by other activities—it's focused time. (Turn off the phones!) Ask your spouse for childhood stories. (Turn off the phones!) Look at old pictures together—this kind of reminiscing often leads to expressing feelings you have never shared, as well as discovering how past moments may have left their impact, for better or for worse. This can also shed light on your reactions to present situations. You will both become more mindful, because you will have availed yourselves of opportunities for the little child within each of you to be heard and understood.

It can be very valuable to get together on a Saturday night or Sunday morning and plan for the coming week. Although it would be perfectly fine while making such plans to throw in some pragmatic appointments and to-dos, it may prove far more significant to devote uninterrupted time each week to taking steps toward accomplishing your shared goals in life.

Your goals are dreams with a deadline. They are your raison d'etre. Yet somehow, however important they may be, they seem to be set aside in favor of all those urgent little chores, like buying printer paper on sale or that trip to Home Depot. Your shared goals are the pillars upon which your marriage rests. Don't put them on the back burner and forget about them. Review your goals and values together often, so you are focused and passionate in a mutual or at least a mutually respectful direction. Write a mission statement (see chapter 15) alone or in tandem, and read it out loud in the morning so you can be more discriminating about the activities that fill your day. If they are not consistent with your goals and values, they can probably be minimized, ignored, or passed along to someone else to handle.

13

Social Skills:
The Power of Positive Speech

Another important building block is positive talk. Earlier I mentioned avoiding judgmental or cynical messages; but let's take it a step further. Positive talk is empowering, affirming, graceful, endearing, and inspiring. We love to surround ourselves with cheerful, upbeat people, so it follows that we should put forth every effort to be like those people: speaking positively, optimistically, and always with a smile. Ask a lot of questions to show that you are deeply interested in what your spouse is thinking or doing. (Not like "Where were you at 10:30 on the night of the 24th?" or "Why can't you put away the tools when you finish with them?")

For those of us who have raised children, recall the difference between a whining child and a smiling child. Then make a conscious decision to emulate the latter. There are times when it's appropriate to address the things that need fixing. But critical conversations are best when sandwiched between expressions of love and broached when we are rested and focused. Try not to complain until you feel certain that it's the right time.

Make a commitment to giving compliments daily. This is not a superficial gesture. Remember the Titanium Rule: "Do not say to your loved ones that which you would not say to a stranger." Each of us needs to heal, to recognize our full potential for aliveness and well-being. Our soul mate silently cries out to us to help him to do just that. For those of you who pray daily from a prayer book, you may note that in our prayers we compliment God repeatedly and tell Him we love Him. Does He need it? No. We do. Similarly, we need to learn to express nurturing words every day to our mate. Speech is a potent gift, given to us to put to good use, and not abuse.

The power of words is inestimable. I firmly believe that some of the greatest contributions to science, literature, and industry happened because someone's spouse told them how important they were that morning, and they went to the office or the laboratory feeling supercharged and empowered. And *presto*—something wonderful was created. It's kind of like the butterfly effect on an emotional level.

Some of the greatest contributions to science, literature, and industry happened because someone's spouse told them how important they were that morning.

Marriage thrives when we establish unity on all four levels: spiritual, intellectual, emotional, and physical. As the only relationship that accomplishes this unity, it must be built on trust. Can you close your eyes and let your spouse lead you through a maze? Can you totally relax and fall backward knowing he will catch you? Can you be candid about what turns you on in the bedroom? These are physical trust building exercises; the emotional counterparts are more elusive. My Waterloo is my backseat driving! I sound like Waze on steroids. I just hope I've given my guy enough positive strokes to overcome this frailty. When you work on saying and doing things that show love, these actions are like deposits in a bank account. Hopefully my paranoid passenger routine will be overshadowed by my loving bank deposits.

How does one build a strong personal bank account? Some couples gain confidence by creating a "Five Things I Like about You" list. Sit down together at the dining room table and write your lists. Then take turns reading them to each other. It may seem a bit contrived at first, but I can tell you that most people who have tried it treasure the compliments and look forward to repeating this exercise.

The WEDS Method, aka the Ten and Ten

Marriage Encounter was a program that first arrived on the scene in the mid-1950s with an extraordinary process that helps couples look deep into their own relationships, through intimate and trusting conversation. Initially presented to members of the Roman Catholic church, it soon became recognized as a universally powerful modality, and was embraced in nondenominational and nonsectarian communities throughout the world. Known as the WEDS method (for reasons that will soon be obvious), it offers couples opportunities to have in-depth, uninterrupted conversations about a topic one or the other feels the need to discuss. It goes something like this.

Write. Each of you sits in a quiet spot and writes a letter in the form of a question, addressing a mutually agreed upon topic, for ten minutes. As you write, keep in mind that you are directing your thoughts to your spouse. Write for the full ten minutes. Begin by answering the question yourself, sharing your own thoughts in two or three sentences. Then, reflecting on your answer, take some additional time to get in touch with your feelings about what you wrote. Write your feelings down, honestly, openly, and sincerely, in a manner that you think your spouse will understand.

Exchange. Come together and lovingly exchange your letters. Try to do so without speaking. Frame this exchange as a ritual, a sacred gift to each other from your essence. Silently read the letter you have just received, then read it again—once for the head and once for the heart.

Dialogue. After you have read the letters twice, discuss your respective feelings. Sit closely together and give each other your full attention. Perhaps hold hands, or sit knee to knee. Then decide which was the strongest feeling from your two letters. Dialogue on that feeling for ten minutes. Once you have exhausted all the ways to describe the feeling, or when ten minutes are up, the dialogue should be brought to closure. At that point, commit to a mutual understanding that you won't bring this up again, not today, or even tomorrow. This is meant to give each of you the time to reflect upon and internalize your spouse's thoughts and feelings. By agreeing not to revisit the issue for a couple of days, you are both working on the powerful tool of impulse control in your relationship. Sometimes oversharing your feelings with your spouse can be disastrous, either because of bad timing or because you've simply talked the topic to death.

Select. While still in a relaxed and mindful state of mind, take another moment to select a question for the next day's dialogue. The ongoing nature of the dialogue is designed to be encouraging—exciting, even—to you both. Don't delay, or it may not happen. Take turns selecting questions and choose topics that are pertinent to your relationship.

Avoid sarcasm. In my house we say, "Kidding causes tension." Humor is great, but not at your soul mate's expense. Your empowering words offer opportunities to overpower your soul mate's inner critic, not to mention your own, allowing the two of you to flourish and prosper. Insensitive remarks, even in jest, may hinder that success. TV shows and other kinds of pop culture displaying an abundance of derogatory humor and sarcasm between spouses are almost as destructive in today's marital milieu as the adventures of glamorous adulterers. Those of us who grew up on *Father Knows Best* and *Ozzie and Harriet* could have predicted the endangerment of the American marriage when the new wave of mean-spirited situation comedies hit the airwaves. Highly evolved, loving relationships are built on respect and trust. Cheap shots that lower your spouse's self-image—amusing though they may be—run counter to the sanctity of your relationship and a loving marriage.

Actions Speak Louder than Words—Sometimes

Service, as we mentioned earlier, is one of the five languages of love. Doing things for your spouse gives a clear message that you care. The day is short, the to-do lists are long, and the demands on your time and attention are many. Bring them little things that show that you're thinking about them, from pistachio nuts to a handmade gift. This morning I woke up to a chocolate mint candy on my pillow.

Touch is another language, and it can create an amazing bond. When it's appropriate, reach for her hand, or give him a hug when he walks in the door. Walk up behind her and surprise her with a kiss. Sadly, when stress levels are high, many people are less affectionate—precisely the opposite of what works to bring a little mellowness to the table. This, from the Touch Research Institute in Florida:

> More than fifty studies indicate massage has positive effects on conditions from colic to hyperactivity to diabetes to migraines. . . . Touch is a means of communication so critical that its absence retards growth in infants.
>
> When we say that somebody touches us emotionally, it means he or she has gone to the core of our being. Physical touch, too, is more than skin-deep. Skin is the human body's largest organ, containing millions of receptors—about 8,000 in a single fingertip—that send messages through nerve fibers to the spinal cord and then to the brain. A simple touch—a hand on a shoulder, an arm around a waist—can reduce the heart rate and lower blood pressure. Positive, nurturing touch appears to stimulate the release of endorphins,

the body's natural pain suppressors. That may explain why a mother's hug can literally "make it better" when a child skins his knee.

Meals too can be either a source of comfort or a source of tension. Try to present them attractively, with consideration for what your spouse enjoys, and on time. It's more important than we imagine. The average person thinks about food 228 times a day. (Don't ask me how they arrived at that statistic, but it sounds about right.) Make sure to eat at least one meal a day as a couple, without distractions, and accompanied by pleasant conversation. Some couples like to plan the week's meals together—anything we plan in writing becomes much easier to implement—and perhaps take turns with food prep and shopping.

Be specific about your expectations concerning responsibilities in the home. If you resent the fact that he isn't more helpful in the kitchen but never express it, that is your issue, not his. If you would like her to spend less time on the laundry and more time on beautiful meals, tell her. Then brainstorm about practical ways to make that happen. You might have to iron your own shirts if you want home-baked bread and fresh soup for dinner. Most spouses want to give, but they're not psychics. They don't necessarily know what you want or need. So say it, without emotion or judgment, and watch things begin to change.

Being a perfect homemaker isn't a fair expectation, but minimally, keep the living room neat and make the beds. Let him walk into an uncluttered environment at the end of a tiring day. And gentlemen, please make sure that your mess isn't in her space.

Finally, make an effort to look good at home. Getting older doesn't mean getting sloppier. Check yourself out in the mirror. Guys, is your hair combed and your shirt on straight? Throw away the sweatpants with a hole in the most uncomplimentary place. Ladies, put on a little lipstick and a squirt of perfume (not the one that smells like a computer). Keep a well-stocked wardrobe of feminine nightwear.

When you think someone is important, you want to make a good impression on them. If you walk around the house looking unkempt or uncared for, you are putting out a subtle message that you don't really think your partner is important or worthy of your honor. Even so, while looking dazzling is a plus, remember *he cares more about the way you look at him than the way you look.*

Givers Are Happier People

The Hebrew word "natan" means to give. It's a palindrome—meaning that it is spelled the same way backwards or forwards. One implication of this is that to give is to receive.

—TAL BEN-SHAHAR, *HAPPINESS STUDIES*

Hone your emotional intelligence to become kinder and more generous. A giving spirit makes for lasting bonds and creates a spiral of good feelings. Research shows that when we spend money on ourselves, the good feeling lasts for a few hours, but when we spend money on others, the good feeling can last for several days. When we give, we like ourselves better, producing endorphins and encouraging us to be yet more giving. This in turn creates an ever-increasing sense of well-being, which encourages us to give even more. So be a giver. And examine what you expect others to do for you that you could be doing on your own. Learn to feel good about yourself for giving praise and compliments without requiring them from others.

Learn to give without expecting a thank-you. An unhappy client came to me complaining bitterly about her ungrateful family. She spent significant time and energy searching for wholesome, delicious recipes, shopping, chopping, stirring, and serving. But nobody complimented her on the food, and no one said, "Thank you." She told me a story she had read about an embittered homemaker who also felt so resentful and angry, she served her loved ones a platter of Kibbles 'n Bits. Her family was shocked when they saw the dog food on the table and assured her that they had always really enjoyed her cooking.

I asked her how she might deal with her family without resorting to Kibbles 'n Bits. "I could teach my family the importance of saying thank you," she said, "and showing appreciation for what others do." She thought of posting an appreciation chart, with space for praise for her husband and kids too for jobs well done. She acknowledged that she could stand to be more transparent, vulnerable, and authentic—simply saying, "I work hard. I need to feel your appreciation." She admitted that she often suppressed her feelings, resulting in things bothering her even more. And it occurred to her that she might have a conversation with herself, recognizing her own creative culinary craft and how rewarding it can be to watch her healthy, happy children grow.

Taking time to validate ourselves can be a great tonic. When we pat ourselves on the back, we are encouraged to accomplish more, to reach for greater heights. That's where those daily small victories noted in your VeGGies journal really pay off. You become more aware of your wins than your losses. Make a habit of looking in the mirror and finding one thing about yourself that you just love. Much of this book is about developing such inward-facing insight; here I want to remind you of how fundamental self-love can be to the quality of all your outer relationships.

Consider the guy whose self-talk is all about how he resents the sacrifices he must make for his family and how unappreciated he feels. If he were to make an effort to reframe his resentment and see his "sacrifice" as a privilege, he might recognize it as a *calling*—part and parcel of his *purpose*. When he works to support his children's education, or to put bread on the table, or so that his wife can live in comfort and security, he's serving, not sacrificing. If his life were all about personal pleasure, who would he be? Remember that only 10 percent of our happiness is based on the situations in which we find ourselves. The other 90 percent is determined by the way we interpret them.

Give, and give some more. Don't worry about being too selfless. Be "self-full." We were all created with a purpose. Actualizing that purpose is a privilege, not a punishment. If Mr. Nobodyappreciatesme were to compose a mission statement that expresses his sense of purpose, perhaps he would appreciate himself more and be less needy of validation from his wife and kids.

A Relaxation Practice

We'll speak more about mission statements later. For now, I want to share a lovely meditation I learned while studying for my certification as a happiness coach. It's a version of a widely known technique—progressive relaxation—but applied in a somewhat deeper dimension.

Sit or lie down in a comfortable position. Imagine a string attached to the top of your head, gently pulling on and extending your spine, so your back becomes straighter and your neck is elongated. Close your eyes and concentrate on your breath. Calm, long exhales, deep, calm inhale . . .

Place your attention on one part of your body at a time, focusing on it as you inhale, and as you exhale, relaxing and releasing any tension in that area. Begin with your head and face. Inhale focusing on your head and face; exhale, relaxing your head and face. Inhale, focusing on your neck, shoulders, and arms, and as you exhale, relax your neck and shoulders and arms. With the next inhale, focus on your chest, your midsection, and your back. As you exhale, relax all the muscles in your chest, your middle, and your back.

Now focus on your lower body, from your pelvis to the tips of your toes. Exhale completely, relaxing the lower section of your body, Surrender. Unplug.

Now return to concentrating on your breath. As you breathe in, you are breathing in light; as you exhale, you are sending light out into the world around you. You are a giver. You take light in, and then you spread light out into the world. To spread it, you must first ingest it. There is no contradiction between selfish and selfless. Enhancing your well-being isn't being self-absorbed—it's making yourself sustainable. Nor is it foolish to increase in generosity. We receive and give, inhale and exhale, contract and expand. Such are the ways of life and interaction: yin and yang, feminine and masculine. Like the chambers of the heart that nourish the entire body and fill it with life. Ask yourself, "What can I do today to be more of a giver?" And now, with the next exhale, open your eyes.

Never Leave Home without a QTIP!

No one can make you feel inferior without your consent.

—Eleanor Roosevelt

Imagine this uncomfortable scenario. You step into a room full of friends, all dressed up, feeling stunning, excited to see and be seen by everyone. As you walk over to two of your besties, Gail and Jason, they move closer to each another and continue their conversation without acknowledging you. You're shocked. You bristle. Your racing thoughts tell you that you were intentionally and brutally snubbed. You walk away feeling alienated, injured. You spend the rest of the evening absolutely miserable.

Time to pick up your QTIP. It's an acronym for *Quit Taking It Personally*. Let's replay the scene from Gail and Jason's perspective. Gail had had a terrible argument with her teenage daughter. She said some things she wished she could take back. When she walked into the party looking glum, Jason, also a parent of teens, asked her why she looked so glum. Reluctantly, Gail opened up and told him the whole story. That was when you walked in. You were ready to party, but they weren't. In fact, they were hardly aware of your presence, because they were so busy unraveling Gail's dilemma. It had nothing to do with you! But your imagination and your wounded ego made it all about you. You might not have an issue with thinking less of yourself if you think about yourself less.

You might not have an issue with thinking less of yourself if you think about yourself less.

Similar situations occur throughout life. A tired husband, a bullied child, an overwhelmed clerk in the grocery store, and our imagination and ego can make it all about us. Check in with the people around you. Can you be present enough to intuit that they might need some space right now? Or at least a knowing smile or hug? Maybe even a latte? The people you depend on for validation are each walking around with their own internal bruises and confusion and tugs-of-war. Your friend might not be emotionally available the moment you need her. In fact, she might really need you. A teacher I greatly admire, Rabbi Manis Friedman, says "The theme is to be needed, rather than to be needy. That's why you are here."

14

Forgiveness

Forgiveness is not an occasional act; it is a permanent attitude.
—MARTIN LUTHER KING JR.

In the worlds of medicine and mental and emotional health, forgiveness has become a widespread topic of discussion.

Fred Luskin, PhD, director of the Stanford University Forgiveness Project, authored the book *Forgive for Good*, a comprehensive study of the effects of forgiving. According to Luskin's findings, forgiveness can improve mental as well as physical well-being. Forgiveness leads to a reduction of the negative effects of stress, and fewer health problems overall. Inability to forgive, on the other hand, may be a more significant risk factor for heart disease than overt hostility. People who chronically blame others for their troubles have higher incidences of such illnesses as cardiovascular disease and cancer. Luskin found that even *imagining* holding a grudge produces negative changes in blood pressure, muscle tension, and immune response, while imagining forgiving someone who has hurt you results in immediate improvement in these same signs.

According to Luskin, one who practices the art of forgiveness becomes "a hero instead of a victim. Forgiveness helps you take control of your feelings. Forgiveness is a choice, a teachable skill, like learning to throw a baseball. Everyone can learn to forgive."

Forgiveness is a choice, a teachable skill, like learning to throw a baseball.

Yet forgiveness is not the same as forgetting, ignoring, or condoning bad behavior. It does not necessarily entail reconciling with the offending party; nor does it demand abandoning one's feelings. In other words, learning how to forgive does not change the fact that the people we forgive remain accountable for their misdeeds.

Forgiving Others

Taking a page from the ethical teachings of an earlier age, contemporary psychology and the self-help literature it inspires have suggested that a perceived offense may be regarded as a *favor*. The best way to respond to a seemingly unforgivable wrong may well be to reframe it as an opportunity, a lesson you need to learn, something your soul needs to reach its full potential. Your adversary may in fact be holding up a mirror to your own weakness or showing you a path to greater inner strength. We can overcome our grievances by understanding how everything that happens to us is for the good. One of my spiritual teachers says, "G-d doesn't do it *to* you. He does it *for* you."

In the words of Viktor Frankl, who was a Holocaust survivor: "Everything can be taken from a man but one thing: the last of the human freedoms—to choose one's attitude in any given set of circumstances, to choose one's own way." The choices we make can be rooted in either a positive or a negative perspective. They can be based on an attitude that sees the universe as random, capricious, or despotic—or we can choose to envision and appreciate the Source of life as loving, generous, and benevolent. And understand that we are loved, collectively and individually, each of us cherished as an only child.

Change your interpretation of the evidence by exercising your good will. Create new evidence. Maybe the person who slighted you was in physical pain, or things were really tough at home; maybe he didn't realize his actions would upset you. You can overcome the momentum and change direction with an act of kindness. Let it go, shake it off, and set yourself free. Cast a new stone and watch for its ripples in the ocean of existence.

Why would a healthy person give over his attention and his waking thoughts to someone who has done him harm? Why rent space in our consciousness to someone who has slandered or insulted us? The inevitable consequences of their offenses that they'll eventually have to face are not in our purview. Their rectification is not our job.

When I was going through the pangs of divorce, I would review my husband's shortcomings on an hourly basis. Divorce wasn't part of my blueprint for a good life. Being divorced didn't jibe with my dreams or my self-image. I was conflicted; thoughts and emotions whipped about as though on a fast-moving roller coaster with no safety harness. Against the advice of my therapist, spiritual mentor, and friends, I convinced myself that to achieve some sort of clarity and feel OK, I needed to go through this constant review.

However, it wasn't a total loss. After I arrived at some measure of clarity, my next job was to let go of my bitterness over all prior offenses, and even to wish my former husband well. He was the father of my amazing children, and we had spent many good years together.

Colin Tipping, author of *Radical Forgiveness*, suggests an effective technique for letting go of the offenses of the past. Write a "release letter" that proclaims to your Higher Self that you give full permission for all aspects of resentment to be lovingly released: "I do hereby forgive _____. I release him to his highest good and set him free. I bless him for having been willing to be my teacher."

There is a prayer in the Jewish tradition that is said every night before bed. To paraphrase it: "Master of the Universe, I hereby forgive anyone who has harmed me, physically, financially, or emotionally, intentionally, or unintentionally, in this incarnation or any other. May no one be punished on my account. And may I not commit the same mistakes as yesterday, and may I learn that in a pleasant way."

After I say this, I feel less anxious, and then I take a minute to envision something I look forward to tomorrow. It helps my sleep, and it surely helps my overall feeling of wellness. In the morning, the first thing I do before I get out of bed is to audibly thank my Divine Source for granting me another day. I set an intention that it will be positive and productive. This kind of reframing only takes a minute. Remember that small changes applied consistently over time make a big difference!

Forgiving Yourself

When you forgive, you in no way change the past,
but you sure do change the future.
—Bernard Meltzer, radio host of *What's Your Problem?*

The forgiveness methods taught by Luskin or cited in self-help books and prayer books can also serve as instruments of self-forgiveness. They help us recognize and reframe our own negative traits and behaviors as opportunities to learn and grow. It can be constructive to look back and learn from our mistakes; it's wise to take precautions to not repeat them in the future.

For some of us, however, forgiving ourselves is even more difficult than forgiving others. When we review the past, we may be filled with paralyzing shame or remorse. Often the desire to change immobilizes us more than it motivates us, as we stay stuck with the indignity of our past misdeeds. The inner critic distorts our perspective and constrains our feelings toward the future. While things are going well, calm prevails. But make a mistake—perhaps something as simple as arriving late for an appointment or forgetting an essential item on the to-do list—and alarms go off, sending danger signals racing to the brain, triggering a flight-or-fight flood of adrenaline. Suddenly all our blunders and personal failures flash before our eyes as though underlined with that bright yellow highlighter that distracts us from past victories. We need to take conscious steps to counteract this syndrome. If we can highlight our wins instead of our losses, we can develop the neural pathways of good memory—the revamped habit of remembering the good.

Here are some affirmations that are particularly effective in such situations:

- I'm doing the best I can with the tools I have.
- The Universe is unfolding exactly as it should.
- Every step forward is a victory. Every smile is a victory.
- Every positive act and thought is a victory!
- God doesn't give me any tests I can't handle.
- This is a test, not a punishment; some of the greatest people in history experienced pain.
- It's difficult, not life-threatening.
- How will I feel about this in five years?

Attach one or more of those affirmations to three deep breaths. It resets your nervous system and reminds you to be solution oriented rather than emotion oriented. You can also associate a sense of calm with a place on your body. Imagine yourself in flow, as in a specific situation in the past when you met with success. Relive it; give it colors and scents. Now choose a point on your body to connect with that good feeling. Massage that place as you reexperience the feeling of wellness. My calm space is between my thumb and my pointer in that soft pocket with no name I know. As I remember feeling in flow, I massage my calm space, and it triggers a sense of well-being.

Journaling about the repressed hurt or shame is another good alternative. Again, there can be events where the pain is so overwhelming it requires professional intervention: abuse, violence, sudden deaths, major illnesses, and divorce, to name a few. Although journaling about those things will clarify your perspective and maybe even tame the terror to a certain extent, a stronger intervention is often called for.

15

Mission Accomplished!

By now you have probably figured out that I have read just about every self-help book that has ever come my way. I've been doing this for forty years. Some were amazing, others were duds, but I never felt that I was wasting time. There was always something to think about, something to grow with. My mission was to keep getting better. Not better than someone else, but better than I was yesterday. My calling is to share what I have learned with the people around me, particularly with parents and educators who are holding the next generation in their hands, but really with anyone who will listen. I branded myself the Getting Better Coach, and I love the lyrics to that classic Beatles tune: "I've got to admit it's getting better, getting so much better all the time."

A certain editor reviewed this book in its early stages and said it sounded like a term paper. How many other peoples' ideas could I possibly borrow, especially from the well-worn works of such giants as Stephen Covey and Viktor Frankl? At the time I took it as something of a slap in the face, but in fact that has been precisely my intent, my challenge: can I take forty years of research and "me-search" and come up with something so coherent and doable that anyone could read it in a few hours and put it to work? And from then on, I hope, spend months and years in action, using habit stacking, rituals, journals, and any or all the other myriad methods I've offered here, and make these insights a part of your life.

Perhaps the best way to integrate all these techniques is to compose a personal mission statement.

Ten years ago, I composed a mission statement. It was agonizing work, because there is a part of me that wants to be everything to everybody. That sometimes drains my energy and dilutes my effectiveness. So I realized I needed to separate the wheat from the chaff, to lighten my load and penetrate to the core of my passion. What makes me tick? What am I willing to stand for? What gives me juice and makes my life worth living? Why do I want to get out of bed in the morning? Who am I really?

What gives me juice and makes my life worth living? Why do I want to get out of bed in the morning? Who am I really?

There's a short version and a long version, and I use them both as yardsticks to help determine how I spend my time and energy. I don't know who said, "There is time in life for everything." Maybe it was Abraham Lincoln. He walked three miles to the library to return two cents that weren't rightfully his. Honesty is one of my core values, but I doubt I'd ever have decided I had time for that. There are lots of things that make sense, but that realistically I just don't have the bandwidth for, and that can bring a lot of unnecessary stress and confusion. I don't need that. How about you?

And so I use my carefully crafted mission statements as the roadmaps to my daily activities. Here's the short version.

Putting wisdom to work: effectively inspiring and empowering myself and others toward tangible personal transformation.

I cultivate presence of mind, purposeful habits, social and emotional intelligence, and harmonious relationships.

I practice loving-kindness, respect, compassion, persistence, gratitude, creativity, and joy.

I am receptive to Divine Wisdom and conscious of Divine Unity.

I am getting better all the time.

I don't always live up to my expectations. But I am capable of picking myself up, brushing away the dust (if not scrubbing away the grime), and beginning again. When we reach for the stars, we may not always get one, but nor will we come up with handfuls of mud. Just today as I was writing these words, my daughter called for the fourth time in a very short span of time, interrupting my train of thought, and challenging the balance among the core values I strive to maintain. Suffice it to say that my response did not epitomize loving-kindness, respect, or compassion. I will call her shortly to apologize for my irritated tone and return to being true to my values.

Note also that my mission statement isn't all about me. Your calling is always bigger than you are. It's about being needed rather than needy. It guides and motivates you to take a responsible place in your family, community, and universe, while using your personal toolbox, fully furnished with multiple talents and techniques, in pursuit of a singular, unique passion.

My longer mission statement starts off the same as the abbreviated one, but it's more practical, and encompasses Tal Ben-Shahar's five SPIRE elements discussed earlier in this book. Wholeness, well-being, or more simply, happiness, is a product of **S**piritual wellness, **P**hysical wellness, **I**ntellectual wellness, **R**elational wellness, and **E**motional wellness. I wrote this mission statement before becoming certified in Tal Ben-Shahar's Happiness Studies, but it seems to have covered all the bases. You'll notice that even though I explicitly express my focus on four out of these five aspects of life, I identify first as a loving wife and an engaged matriarch of an extraordinary family. That covers the fifth aspect, relational wellness. Some of the longer version of the mission statement is repetitive, and for that I apologize, but Tal would tell us that repetition, as in reminders and rituals, enables us to effect real change and build new habits.

I effectively inspire and influence others and myself toward tangible personal transformation.

I cultivate presence of mind, purposeful habits, social and emotional intelligence, and harmonious relationships.

I practice loving-kindness, respect, compassion, persistence, gratitude, creativity, and joy.

I am receptive to Divine Wisdom and conscious of Divine Unity.

I am a loving wife and an actively engaged matriarch of an extraordinary family.

I continually renew myself by focusing on the four aspects of my life:

Physical: *My commitment to daily exercise and healthy eating keeps me strong and well.*

Emotional: Through daily meditation, regular entries in my gratitude journal, and intentional choices of positive thoughts and language, I attain inner calm, a trusting temperament, and I make the space to do the things I enjoy.

Intellectual: Through meaningful reading, lectures, and workshops, my knowledge and wisdom grow ever broader.

Spiritual: The specific blocks of time I devote each day to prayer, learning, and good deeds lead me to a 24/7 connectedness to my Source, expanding awareness and benevolence toward the world.

I am getting better all the time.

As I'm planning my week, my day, or deciding how I'll spend that spare hour in the evening, I check in with my mission statement to confirm whether a given activity fits. With time, it becomes more automatic. I just know. Earlier, I mentioned people who become great by doing what they are good at rather than spending months or years trying to perfect those things that are difficult for them. The latter might be an honorable modus operandi for some, but it won't necessarily lead to happiness or excellence. My mission statement reflects what I am good at and how I can create more goodness in the world through my personal strengths and values.

Writing Your Mission Statement

Draft a list of the core values and strengths that define you. Connect that to your calling or your dream of who you will be in five years. Write it and rewrite it until it flows. That is your mission statement. It may change next year or even next month, but for now it offers you focus and direction.

Here's a step-by-step guide on how to write a personal mission statement:

1. **Set aside time for reflection.** Find a quiet and comfortable place where you can think and reflect without distractions. Allow ample time for this process.

2. **Identify your values.** Begin by identifying your core values. These are the principles and beliefs that are most important to you. Examples of values include honesty, integrity, family, personal growth, and compassion.

3. **Clarify your passions and interests.** Think about what activities, causes, or areas of life truly excite and motivate you. What are your passions and interests? What makes you feel fulfilled and alive?

4. **Define your strengths and talents.** Reflect on your strengths, talents, and skills. What are you naturally good at? How can you use these abilities to make a positive impact?

5. **Set personal goals.** Consider your short-term and long-term personal goals. What do you want to achieve in various aspects of your life, such as career, relationships, health, and personal development?

6. **Craft your mission statement.** Begin writing your mission statement. Start with a sentence that captures your overarching purpose in life. Be concise and clear in your expression.

7. **Incorporate values and goals.** Integrate your core values into your mission statement. Explain how these values guide your actions and decisions. Also, mention some of your key life goals or aspirations.

8. **Inspire and motivate.** Make your mission statement inspirational and motivational. Use language that resonates in

your heart and soul. It should evoke a sense of purpose and enthusiasm.

9. **Keep it concise.** Aim to keep your mission statement relatively short, ideally a paragraph or two. Avoid making it too lengthy or complex.

10. **Review and revise.** Understand that your personal mission statement is not set in stone. As you grow and evolve, your values and goals may change. Periodically revisit and revise your statement to ensure it remains relevant.

11. **Seek feedback.** Share your personal mission statement with trusted friends, family members, or mentors. They can provide valuable insights and feedback.

12. **Live your mission.** Use your mission statement as a guide in your daily life. Make decisions and take actions that align with your mission and values.

Your personal mission statement should help you make choices that are in harmony with your authentic self and aspirations. Here's a simplified template to help you get started:

"I am committed to [*insert your core purpose*] by [*briefly state how you achieve it*] for [*who is your audience or community*] through [*key activities*]. My actions are guided by my core values of [*list no more than five values*]."

Now you own the tools. The challenge is to open the toolbox and use them. Be receptive to the possibility of growth and change. Remember the importance of repetition and ritual in your effort to make this knowledge a working part of your life. Start a journal and recount your "gratitudes," because what you appreciate, appreciates. Call upon friends and colleagues to support you, and above all support yourself. Remember that small changes applied consistently over time make a big difference. Be OK with being just 1 percent better today than you were yesterday. Give yourself permission to be human, knowing that some days you will fail miserably, but you are not a failure. Dip back into this book again and again with curiosity. At times, one technique will suit your fancy, while other days you will be attracted to something entirely different. Try to find the balance between spontaneity and consistent routine. Remember that while it is human to entertain all emotions and none are inherently bad, happiness and a positive mindset are the most potent vitamins for your success. Enjoy life. Take minivacations every couple of hours, a day off each week, and a month off each year. Breathe deeply and meditate. Sprinkle your days with five-minute workouts. In the immortal words of Thoreau, "Go confidently in the direction of your dreams. Live the life you have imagined."

And now, my friend, go coach yourself!

Suggested Reading

Ben-Shahar, Tal. *Happier: Learn the Secrets to Daily Joy and Lasting Fulfillment*. New York: McGraw Hill, 2007.

——. *Happier No Matter What: Cultivating Hope, Resilience, and Purpose in Hard Times*. New York: The Experiment, 2021.

Benson, Herbert, and Miriam Z. Klipper. *The Relaxation Response*. New York: Harper Collins, 2000.

Buettner, Daniel. *The Blue Zones Secrets for Living Longer: Lessons from the Healthiest Places on Earth*. Washington, D.C.: National Geographic, 2023.

Buncher, Beverly. *BALM: The Loving Path to Family Recovery*. N.p.: Peach Elephant Press, 2018.

Cameron, Julia. *The Artist's Way: A Spiritual Path to Higher Creativity*. New York: Penguin Putnam, 2002 [1986].

Chapman, Gary. *The Five Love Languages: The Secret to Love That Lasts*. Chicago: Northfield Press, 2015.

Clear, James. *Atomic Habits: An Easy and Proven Way to Build Good Habits and Break Bad Ones*. New York: Avery, 2018.

Frankl, Viktor. *Man's Search for Meaning.* Boston: Beacon Press, 1959.

Frederickson, Barbara L. *Love 2.0: Creating Happiness and Health in Moments of Connection.* New York: Plume, 2013.

Gibran, Kahlil. *The Prophet.* New York: Readers' Library Classics, 2022 [1923].

Gottman, John M. *The Seven Principles for Making Marriage Work.* Chatsworth, Calif.: Harmony Press, 2015.

Luskin, Fred. *Forgive for Good.* San Francisco: Harper One, 2001.

Pennebaker, James W. *Opening Up by Writing It Down.* New York: Guilford Press, 2016.

Piper, Watty. *The Little Engine That Could.* New York: Grosset and Dunlap, 2020 [1930].

Schnarch, David. *Passionate Marriage: Keeping Love and Intimacy Alive in Committed Relationships.* London: Scribe, 1999.

Waldinger, Robert, and Marc Schulz. *The Good Life: Lessons from the World's Longest Scientific Study of Happiness.* New York: Simon and Schuster, 2023.

About the Author

Frumma describes herself as "The Coaches' Coach," because at least ten of her clients are top coaches themselves. An early explorer in the fields of Colorado wildflowers and positive psychology, she became a pioneer in the natural food movement in America and a spiritual mentor to many. She has spent the last thirty years sharing her knowledge of emotional intelligence as a beloved educator, personal and relationships coach, teacher-trainer, and popular speaker online and around the world. Frumma lives with her husband Simcha in Florida, where she writes, coaches, swims daily, and enjoys the company of her very large and loving extended family.